The Ultimate Chowder Cookbook

100 Delicious Recipes for Every Taste and Occasion. Classic Comfort Food with Creative Twists, Low-Fat and Vegetarian Options Seafood, Corn, Clam, and Bacon Chowder Recipes

Lily Roberts

TABLE OF CONTENTS

INTRODUCTION

In this cookbook, we've gathered 100 mouthwatering chowder recipes that are perfect for any occasion. Chowders are a classic comfort food that have been enjoyed for generations, and we've included a wide variety of recipes to suit every taste and dietary preference.

Our recipes range from traditional New England clam chowder to spicy Cajun-style seafood chowder, creamy corn chowder to hearty bacon and potato chowder. We've also included creative twists on old favorites, like a sweet potato and bacon chowder or a chicken and corn chowder.

For those who are looking for healthier options, we've included recipes for low-fat and vegetarian chowders that are just as flavorful and comforting as their traditional counterparts.

Each recipe in this cookbook includes step-by-step instructions and beautiful photographs, so you can see exactly what your chowder should look like. We've also included tips and tricks for achieving the perfect consistency and flavor, so you can impress your friends and family with your culinary skills.

Whether you're looking to warm up on a cold winter night, enjoy a bowl of soup for lunch, or impress your guests at your next dinner party, this cookbook has something for everyone. So come along with us on a journey through the world of chowder, and discover the endless possibilities of this classic comfort food..

FISH AND SEAFOOD

1. Canned Clam Chowder soup

Makes: 4-5 jars

INGREDIENTS:
- Salt pork, ½ pound, diced
- Onion, chopped
- 12-16 cups clam, chopped
- 8 cups potatoes, diced and peeled
- 8 cups boiling water
- Salt and pepper, to taste
- 2 cups tomatoes, cooked
- ½ cup celery, chopped
- ½ bay leaf
- ½ tablespoon thyme

INSTRUCTIONS:
a) Prepare the pressure canner. Add water into the pressure canner. Insert the trivet and bring it to a boil on medium heat on the stove. Place empty jars into the simmering water for 5-10 minutes. But, do not boil. When done, keep it aside.
b) Add salt pork into the saucepan and cook until lightly brown.
c) Add onion and cook until tender. Then, add water, potatoes, and clam and bring it to a boil, for about 10 minutes.
d) Place the chowder base into the jars, leaving 1-inch headspace.
e) Remove any air bubbles.
f) Place jars into the pressure canner and process them for 1 hour and 40 minutes.
g) When done, remove jars from the pressure canner.

2. Canned Fish Chowder

Makes: 5 pints

INGREDIENTS:
- 2 pounds fresh fish, boned and skinned
- 6 large tomatoes
- 2 garlic cloves
- 2 teaspoons sugar
- 1/2 teaspoon celery salt
- 1 dash cayenne
- 4 cups peeled and cubed potatoes
- 1/2 cup chopped onion
- 1/4 cup chopped pimiento
- 3 slices bacon, crisp-cooked, drained, and crumbled
- 1 tablespoon lemon juice

INSTRUCTIONS:
a) Cut fish into 1 piece.
b) Soak for 1 hour in a brine solution made of 8 cups water and ½ cup salt. Drain fish.
c) Combine 3 cups water, tomatoes, garlic, sugar,1 teaspoon salt, celery salt, and a dash of cayenne.
d) Cover and simmer for 20 minutes. Add remaining ingredients .
e) Bring to a boil, and cook just to heat vegetables. Add Fish. Pack into hot jars, leaving 1-inch headspace.
f) Adjust lids. Process in a pressure canner, at 10 pounds, pints, and quarts 100 minutes.

3. Chunky Fish Chowder

Serving: 8

Ingredients

3 bacon strips, diced

1 large onion, chopped

1 garlic clove, minced

1 can (14-1/2 ounces) stewed tomatoes

4 cups water

3/4 teaspoon ground cumin

1/2 teaspoon salt

1/4 teaspoon ground turmeric

Dash pepper

2 medium potatoes, peeled and diced

1 pound cod, cut into 3/4-inch pieces

1 package (10 ounces) frozen whole kernel corn, thawed

1 tablespoon cider vinegar

GARLIC BUTTER:

1/2 cup butter, softened

2 tablespoons chopped fresh parsley

2 tablespoons lemon juice

2 garlic cloves, minced

Fish-shaped crackers, optional

Direction

a) Cook the bacon in a large saucepan until it turns brown and crispy.

b) Take off from heat and set aside using a slotted utensil.

c) Using the same pan, cook the garlic and onion in the bacon fat until they turn tender. Stir in water, pepper, turmeric, salt, tomatoes, and cumin and allow to boil. Add in the potatoes and simmer for 15 minutes or until the potatoes become tender.

d) Add in vinegar, fish, and corn; let cook until the fish becomes easily flake with a fork or for about 10 minutes. Stir in the reserved bacon.

e) To make the garlic butter, whip garlic, parsley, lemon juice, and butter in a small container until it becomes fluffy. Serve the soup with a dollop of garlic butter on top; include crackers if desired.

4. Coconut Milk Conch Chowder

INGREDIENTS:
- 1 lb. conch meat
- 1/4 cup cooking oil, divided
- 2 green onions, chopped
- 1 carrot, diced
- 1 stalk celery, diced
- 1 small red bell pepper, diced
- ½ fresh corn kernels
- 2 tablespoons all-purpose flour
- 1-quart half and half
- 14-ounce can of coconut milk
- 2 cups fish stock
- 1 ½ tablespoons grated fresh ginger root
- Salt and pepper to taste
- 1 ½ teaspoon hot sauce
- 1 bunch of fresh cilantro (coriander), chopped

INSTRUCTIONS:
a) Place conch meat in a pot with enough water to cover and bring to a boil. Cook for 15 minutes.

b) Drain and finely chop.

c) Melt 2 tablespoons of oil in a skillet over medium heat and mix in the green onions, carrots, celery, red pepper, and corn. Cook and stir for 5 minutes.

d) Melt the remaining 2 tablespoons of oil in a large pot and whisk in the flour to create a roux. Pour in the half and half, coconut milk, and fish stock. Mix in the ginger and season with salt and pepper.

e) Stir the conch and vegetables into the pot. Bring to a boil, reduce heat to low, and simmer for 15 minutes. Mix in the hot sauce and cilantro (coriander). Continue cooking for 15 minutes, or to desired consistency.

5. Shrimp and pumpkin chowder

Makes: 4 servings

INGREDIENTS
- 2 onions, sliced
- 2 carrots, thinly sliced
- 1 tablespoon snipped fresh cilantro
- 2 teaspoons grated fresh ginger
- 2 cloves garlic, minced
- ½ teaspoon ground allspice
- 2 tablespoons olive oil
- 14-ounce can of chicken broth
- 15-ounce can of pumpkin
- 1½ cups Reduced Fat Milk
- 8-ounce package of frozen, peeled, and deveined cooked shrimp, thawed
- Fresh shrimp in shells, peeled, deveined, and cooked
- Snipped fresh chives

INSTRUCTIONS
a) Cook the onions, carrots, cilantro, ginger, garlic, and allspice in heated oil in a saucepan over medium heat for 14 minutes, or until the veggies are soft.
b) Transfer the mixture to the bowl of a food processor.
c) Add½ cup of chicken broth.
d) Process until almost smooth.
e) Combine the pumpkin, milk, and remaining broth in the same saucepan.
f) Add the 8 ounces of shrimp and the combined vegetable mixture, and cook through.
g) Pour the soup into the dishes.
h) Garnish with chopped chives.

6. Clam, Shrimp, and Crab Chowder

Makes: 10 Servings

INGREDIENTS

- ½ pound bacon, chopped
- 1 large yellow onion, diced
- 2 medium carrots, peeled and diced
- 2 stalks celery, diced
- 2½ cups seafood stock
- 2 large red potatoes, peeled and diced
- 3 garlic cloves, minced
- ¾ cup (1½ sticks) salted butter
- ¾ cup all-purpose flour
- 2 cups heavy cream
- 2 cups whole milk
- 1 cup minced clams
- ½ cup crab meat
- 2 teaspoons kosher salt
- 1 teaspoon ground black pepper
- ½ pound medium raw shrimp, peeled and deveined
- 2 tablespoons chopped fresh parsley

INSTRUCTIONS

a) Toss the bacon into a large stockpot, and turn the heat to medium. Cook the bacon until it is crisp. Then remove it from the pot, reserving the fat in the pot, and set the bacon to the side.

b) Add the onion, carrot, and celery to the pot. Cook until they are nice and tender, then pour in the seafood stock. Add the potatoes and garlic, and simmer for about 15 minutes, still on medium heat.

c) While that's cooking, in a medium saucepan, add the butter and melt it over medium heat. Sprinkle in the flour and whisk. Cook for 3 minutes, stirring continuously, then pour in the cream and milk. Be sure to whisk so it's lump-free!

d) Pour the butter-and-flour mixture into the large pot with the other ingredients, and stir. Add the clams, crab, salt, and black pepper. Mix the ingredients, then reduce the heat to low.

e) Add the shrimp and bacon, and stir. Simmer for 15 minutes. Top off with fresh parsley before serving.

7. Fish Chowder

Makes: 8

INGREDIENTS:
- 32 ounces can diced tomatoes
- 2 tablespoons olive oil
- ¼ cup chopped celery
- ½ cup fish stock
- ½ cup white wine
- 1 cup spicy V8 juice
- 1 chopped green bell pepper
- 1 chopped onion
- 4 minced garlic cloves
- Salt the pepper to taste
- 1 teaspoon Italian seasoning
- 2 peeled and sliced carrots
- 2 ½ pounds cut-up tilapia
- ½ pounds peeled and deveined shrimp

INSTRUCTIONS:
a) In your large pot, heat the olive oil first.
b) Cook the bell pepper, onion, and celery for 5 minutes in a hot skillet.
c) After that, add the garlic. Cook for 1 minute after that.
d) In a large mixing bowl, combine all remaining ingredients except the seafood.
e) Cook the stew for 40 minutes on low heat.
f) Add the tilapia and shrimp and stir to combine.
g) Simmer for an additional 5 minutes.
h) Taste and adjust the seasoning before serving.

8. New England Clam Chowder

INGREDIENTS:

- 6–7 slices bacon, cut into small pieces
- 3 tablespoons flour
- 1 pound red or yellow potatoes
- 1 cup heavy cream
- 1 medium white onion, diced
- 1 cup milk, divided
- 1 (10-oz) can whole baby clams
- 1 cup Chicken Bone Broth, divided
- 2 stalks of celery, finely chopped
- 3 tablespoons unsalted butter
- 1 teaspoon dill weed
- salt and pepper to taste

INSTRUCTIONS:

a) In a medium saucepan, cook bacon over medium heat until crispy. Stir occasionally (about 10 minutes).

b) While the bacon is cooking, make cream of celery Broth Soup. In a medium skillet, melt butter over medium heat. Add ¼ cup chopped onion and sauté until fragrant (3-5 minutes).

c) Add celery into the skillet; stir and cook for 2-3 minutes.

d) Sprinkle with flour and sauté with onion and celery for a minute or two.

e) Whisk in ½cup whole milk and ½cup chicken broth. Bring to a simmer and cook for 5-8 minutes until it's thickened.

f) While the cream of celery Broth Soup is simmering, the bacon should be ready. Stir in the rest of the onion into the saucepan and cook until translucent.

g) Add the juice from the clams and ½cup chicken broth, followed by potatoes. Cover and cook over medium heat until potatoes are fork tender (about 15-20 minutes). Stir occasionally.

h) While potatoes are cooking, check and complete the cream of celery Broth Soup.

i) Once the potatoes are done, add clams, cream of celery Broth Soup, ½cup milk, heavy cream and dill weed. Stir everything together consistently and cook the chowder over medium-low heat for another 5 minutes. Season with salt and pepper to taste. Serve.

9. Wholesome Fish Chowder

INGREDIENTS:

- 1 pound tilapia fillet
- 1 pound yellow potatoes
- 12 ounces carrots
- 1 small bunch of fresh cilantro
- ½ cup white onion, chopped
- 8 cups Chicken Bone Broth (4 cartons)
- Olive oil, salt and pepper
- 2 teaspoons Old Bay Seasoning
- Lemon wedges for serving

INSTRUCTIONS:

a) Preheat oven to 350°F. Thaw fish and pat dry with a paper towel. Brush fish with olive oil. Sprinkle a dash of salt and pepper on each fillet.

b) Lay prepared fish fillets in a baking dish without overlap. Bake for 14 minutes.

c) While fish is baking, add chicken bone broth in a large saucepan and bring to a rapid boil.

d) Peel and chop up carrots and potatoes. Place them in the boiling bone broth, then reduce heat to medium-high. Cover to cook for 15 minutes or until the vegetables are tender.

e) Transfer vegetables and just enough broth into a blender, add cilantro and onion, and blend for 10 seconds or until smooth. Now you've made a wholesome chowder base.

f) Return chowder base into the same saucepan.

g) Use a fork to break cooked fish into small pieces and transfer fish pieces into the chowder base.

h) Add Old Bay Seasoning and stir well. Simmer for 5 more minutes over medium heat.

i) Serve with a squeeze of lemon juice and toasted bread.

10. Salmon Vegetable Chowder

Servings: 4 servings

INGREDIENTS:
- 2 salmon fillets, skin removed and cut into bite-size pieces
- 1 ½ cups white onion, finely chopped
- 1 ½ cups sweet potato, peeled and diced
- 1 cup broccoli florets, cut into small pieces
- 3 cups chicken broth
- 2 cups whole milk
- 2 Tablespoons all-purpose flour
- 1 teaspoon dried thyme
- 3 Tablespoons unsalted butter
- 1 bay leaf
- Salt and pepper to taste
- Flat parsley, finely chopped

INSTRUCTIONS:
a) Cook chopped onion in unsalted butter until translucent. Stir in flour and mix well with the butter and onion. Pour in chicken broth and milk, then add sweet potato cubes, bay leaf and thyme.

b) Let the mixture simmer for 5-10 minutes while stirring occasionally.

c) Add the salmon and broccoli florets. Then, cook for 5-8 minutes.

d) Season with salt and pepper and adjust the taste when necessary.

e) Transfer to small individual bowls and garnish with chopped parsley.

11. <u>Salmon and Corn Chowder</u>

- 1 pound salmon fillet
- 2 ears fresh corn
- 2 tablespoons olive oil
- 1 medium finely chopped onion
- 1 medium Yukon gold potato, diced
- 2 cups whole milk
- 1 cup light cream
- 4 tablespoons unsalted butter
- ½ teaspoon Worcestershire sauce
- ¼ cup finely chopped tarragon
- 1 teaspoon paprika
- Salt and freshly ground black pepper
- Oyster crackers

a) Preheat a grill.

b) Lay the salmon and the corncobs on the oiled grill. Cook 6 minutes; then turn and cook 4 to 5 minutes longer. Set aside.

c) With a sharp knife, strip the corn from the cobs and cut the salmon into bite-sized pieces. Set aside.

d) Heat 1 tablespoon of the oil in a 4-quart saucepan over medium-high heat. Add the onion and potato. Cook, covered, for about 10 minutes, or until the onions are soft. Add the milk, cream, butter, and Worcestershire sauce. Simmer for about 10 minutes, or until the potatoes are soft

e) Stir in the corn, salmon, tarragon, paprika, salt, and pepper and simmer for 5 minutes.

f) Transfer to bowls and serve immediately with oyster crackers.

12. John Dory Chowder

Serves 4

- 500g (1lb) mussels, cleaned
- 150ml (¼ pint) Cornish cider
- 25g (1oz) butter
- 100g piece of rindless smoked streaky bacon
- 1 small onion, finely chopped
- 20g (¾oz) plain flour
- 1 litre (1¾ pints) full-cream milk
- 2 potatoes
- 1 bay leaf
- 225g (8oz) John Dory fillet
- 120ml double cream
- pinch of cayenne pepper
- salt and freshly ground white pepper
- 2 tbsp freshly chopped parsley

a) Put the cleaned mussels and cider into a medium-sized pan over a high heat. Cover and cook for 2–3 minutes or until they have just opened, shaking the pan occasionally.

b) Melt the butter in another pan, add the bacon and fry until lightly golden. Add the onion and cook gently for 5 minutes or until the onion has softened.

c) Stir in the flour and cook for 1 minute. Gradually stir in the milk and then add all but the last tablespoon or two of the mussel cooking liquor. Add the potatoes and bay leaf and 1 level teaspoon of salt, and simmer.

d) Remove the bay leaf, add the pieces of John Dory and simmer for 2–3 minutes or until the fish is just cooked. Stir in the double cream.

e) Remove from the heat and stir in the mussels.

13. Clam, Shrimp, and Crab Chowder

YIELD: 10 SERVINGS

INGREDIENTS

½ pound bacon, chopped

1 large yellow onion, diced

2 medium carrots, peeled and diced

2 stalks celery, diced

2½ cups seafood stock

2 large red potatoes, peeled and diced

3 garlic cloves, minced

¾ cup (1½ sticks) salted butter

¾ cup all-purpose flour

2 cups heavy cream

2 cups whole milk

1 cup minced clams

½ cup crab meat

2 teaspoons kosher salt

1 teaspoon ground black pepper

½ pound medium raw shrimp, peeled and deveined

2 tablespoons chopped fresh parsley

DIRECTIONS

Toss the bacon into a large stockpot, and turn the heat to medium. Cook the bacon until it is crisp. Then remove it from the pot, reserving the fat in the pot, and set the bacon to the side.

Add the onion, carrot, and celery to the pot. Cook until they are nice and tender, then pour in the seafood stock. Add the potatoes and garlic, and simmer for about 15 minutes, still on medium heat.

While that's cooking, in a medium saucepan, add the butter and melt it over medium heat. Sprinkle in the flour and whisk. Cook for 3 minutes, stirring continuously, then pour in the cream and milk. Be sure to whisk so it's lump-free!

Pour the butter-and-flour mixture into the large pot with the other ingredients, and stir. Add the clams, crab, salt, and black pepper. Mix the ingredients, then reduce the heat to low.

Add the shrimp and bacon, and stir. Simmer for 15 minutes. Top off with fresh parsley before serving.

14. Salmon and Corn Chowder

Ingredients:

- 1-pound salmon fillet
- 2 ears fresh corn
- 2 tablespoons olive oil
- 1 medium finely chopped onion
- 1 medium Yukon gold potato, diced
- 2 cups whole milk
- 1 cup light cream
- 4 tablespoons unsalted butter
- ½ teaspoon Worcestershire sauce
- ¼ cup finely chopped tarragon
- 1 teaspoon paprika
- Salt and freshly ground black pepper
- Oyster crackers

Directions:

a) Preheat a grill.

b) Lay the salmon and the corncobs on the oiled grill. Cook 6 minutes; then turn and cook 4 to 5 minutes longer. Set aside.

c) With a sharp knife, strip the corn from the cobs and cut the salmon into bite-sized pieces. Set aside.

d) Heat 1 tablespoon of the oil in a 4-quart saucepan over medium-high heat. Add the onion and potato. Cook, covered, for about 10 minutes, or until the onions are soft. Add the milk, cream, butter, and Worcestershire sauce. Simmer for about 10 minutes, or until the potatoes are soft

e) Stir in the corn, salmon, tarragon, paprika, salt, and pepper and simmer for 5 minutes.

f) Transfer to bowls and serve immediately with oyster crackers.

15. Bay scallop chowder

Yield: 12 servings

Ingredient
- 3 tablespoons Butter
- 2 ounces Smoked bacon
- 1 large Onion(s), finely chopped
- 1 large Garlic clove(s), minced
- ½ teaspoon Crushed red pepper
- 6 cups Bottled clam broth
- 6 cups Chicken stock
- 2 Bay leaves
- 5 Parsley sprigs
- 3 Thyme sprigs
- 8 Black peppercorns
- 1½ pounds Yukon Gold potatoes
- 2¼ cup Heavy cream
- 2 tablespoons Cornstarch
- 2 larges Leeks
- 1/8 inch thick
- 1½ pounds Bay scallops
- Salt and pepper
- ¼ cup Chives, finely chopped

Directions

a) Melt the butter in a large enameled cast-iron casserole. Add the bacon and cook over moderately high heat, stirring, until lightly browned, about 2 minutes Add the onion and cook, stirring occasionally, until softened, about 7 minutes Stir in the garlic and crushed red onion(s) and cook, stirring, until the garlic is fragrant, about 2 minutes

b) Add the clam broth, chicken stock, and bouquet garni to the casserole and bring to a boil over high heat. Lower the heat to moderately high and simmer for 20 minutes

c) Add the diced potatoes to the soup and cook over moderately high heat until just tender, about 10 minutes Discard the bouquet garni.

d) In a medium bowl, whisk ¼ cup of the heavy cream with the cornstarch until smooth. Whisk in the remaining 2 cups cream, then whisk the mixture into the soup. Bring the soup to a boil over moderately high heat. Add the leeks and cook until just tender, about 4 minutes

e) Stir the scallops into the chowder and cook over moderate heat just until opaque throughout, 2-3 min; don't let the soup boil. Season with salt and pepper. Ladle the chowder into a tureen or individual bowls. Garnish with the chopped chives and serve at once.

16. Shrimp and pumpkin chowder

Makes: 4 servings

INGREDIENTS
- 2 onions, sliced
- 2 carrots, thinly sliced
- 1 tablespoon snipped fresh cilantro
- 2 teaspoons grated fresh ginger
- 2 cloves garlic, minced
- ½ teaspoon ground allspice
- 2 tablespoons olive oil
- 14-ounce can of chicken broth
- 15-ounce can of pumpkin
- 1½ cups Reduced Fat Milk
- 8-ounce package of frozen, peeled, and deveined cooked shrimp, thawed
- Fresh shrimp in shells, peeled, deveined, and cooked
- Snipped fresh chives

INSTRUCTIONS
a) Cook the onions, carrots, cilantro, ginger, garlic, and allspice in heated oil in a saucepan over medium heat for 14 minutes, or until the veggies are soft.
b) Transfer the mixture to the bowl of a food processor.
c) Add½ cup of chicken broth.
d) Process until almost smooth.
e) Combine the pumpkin, milk, and remaining broth in the same saucepan.
f) Add the 8 ounces of shrimp and the combined vegetable mixture, and cook through.
g) Pour the soup into the dishes.
h) Garnish with chopped chives.

17. Shrimp-And-Fennel Chowder

Makes: 6

INGREDIENTS:
- 2 tablespoons olive oil
- 2 cups thinly sliced fennel
- 1½ cups chopped leek
- 1½ cups chopped celery
- 1 tablespoon minced garlic
- 1 cup dry white wine
- 28-ounce can of no-salt-added fire-roasted diced tomatoes
- 1 russet potato, peeled and cut into ½-inch cubes
- 1 cup water
- 1 cup clam juice
- 1 teaspoon kosher salt
- ⅛ teaspoon saffron threads
- 1 pound raw shrimp, peeled and deveined

INSTRUCTIONS:
a) Heat the oil in a nonstick skillet over moderate heat. Add the fennel, leek, celery, and garlic to the skillet; cook, stirring occasionally until the vegetables are softened and lightly caramelized, 6 to 8 Minutes. Add the wine to the skillet; cook for 1 minute, stirring and scraping to loosen the browned bits from the bottom of the skillet. Transfer the mixture to a Crockpot.
b) Stir the tomatoes, potato, water, clam juice, salt, and saffron threads into the Crockpot. Slow cook, covered, until the potato is tender, 5 to 6 Hours. Increase the Crockpot heat to HIGH; stir in the shrimp.
c) Cover and cook until the shrimp are done, 5 to 7 Minutes. Ladle the chowder into bowls, and serve hot.

18. Haddock, Leek & Potato Chowder

- 1/4 Haddock Fillet
- 25g Sliced Leek
- 25g Herby Diced
- Potato
- 15g Diced Onion
- 250ml Cream
- 100ml Fish Stock
- Chopped Parsley

a) Pan Fry the washed and chopped leek.
b) When the leek has softened add the potato and onion.
c) Once the vegetables are warm add the cream and stock and bring to the boil. Turn down to a simmer and add the chopped haddock.
d) Simmer for 10 minutes and add chopped parsley as you serve.

19. Jamaican shrimp soup

MAKES: 2

INGREDIENTS:
- 2 tablespoons Green Curry Paste
- 1 cup Vegetable Stock
- 1 cup Coconut Milk
- 6 oz. Precooked Shrimp
- 5 oz. Broccoli Florets
- 3 tablespoons Cilantro, chopped
- 2 tablespoons Coconut Oil
- 1 tablespoon Soy Sauce
- Juice of ½ Lime
- 1 medium Spring Onion, chopped
- 1 teaspoon Crushed Roasted Garlic
- 1 teaspoon Minced Ginger
- 1 teaspoon Fish Sauce
- ½ teaspoon Turmeric
- ½ cup Sour Cream

INSTRUCTIONS:
- In a medium-sized saucepan, melt the coconut oil.
- Add the garlic, ginger, spring onions, green curry paste, and turmeric. Add the soy sauce, and fish sauce.
- Cook for 2 minutes.
- Add vegetable stock and coconut milk and stir thoroughly. Cook for a few minutes on low heat.
- Add the broccoli florets and cilantro and stir thoroughly once the curry has thickened a little.
- When you're satisfied with the curry's consistency, add the shrimp and lime juice, and stir everything together.
- Cook for a few minutes on low heat. If necessary, season with salt and pepper.

20. **Stewed Calaloo**

INGREDIENTS:
- Chopped calaloo leaves
- 3 tablespoons of vegetable oil
- 2 minced garlic cloves
- 2 medium onions
- 1 cup Coconut milk
- Salt
- Pepper
- Hot pepper sauce

INSTRUCTIONS:
a) Heat oil in a heavy saucepan. Add chopped onions and garlic. When soft, add calaloo leaves and toss until coated with oil and wilted.

b) Add coconut milk until enough to cover calaloo. Simmer until the calaloo is soft and most of the milk has evaporated.

c) Add seasonings and serve as a vegetable.

21. Coconut Prawn Soup

MAKES: 4

INGREDIENTS:
- 600g of raw prawns, deveined
- 1 small onion chopped
- 2 medium-sized carrots chopped
- 1 red bell pepper chopped
- 2-3 cups of spinach or kale, chopped
- 2 scallion chopped
- a handful of whole okra
- 4 garlic cloves minced
- 1 tablespoon ginger minced
- 1 can of coconut milk
- 1 liter of vegetable stock
- 1 teaspoon of seafood seasoning
- 1 teaspoon of black pepper
- 5 sprigs of fresh thyme
- 2 teaspoons of parsley
- 1 scotch bonnet
- ¼ teaspoon of red chili flakes for heat
- a squeeze of fresh lime juice
- ⅛ teaspoon of Himalayan pink salt
- coconut oil
- 1 tablespoon of tapioca mixed with 2 tablespoons of warm water for a thicker soup

INSTRUCTIONS:
a) Place the prawns into a medium bowl and marinate with the seafood seasoning, then set aside.
b) Melt 2 tablespoons of coconut oil in a large saucepan on medium heat.
c) Proceed to add the onions, scallion, and garlic then sauté until soft and translucent.
d) Add the carrots, garlic, bell peppers, and spinach and continue to cook for 5 minutes

e) Add the black pepper, parsley, thyme, and chili flakes (if using) and stir and combine with the veggies.

f) Pour the vegetable stock and coconut milk into the saucepan then bring to a rolling boil

g) Add the scotch bonnet and then reduce the heat to low with the lid on.

h) Simmer for 20 minutes

i) After 15 minutes, add the okra and prawns and stir in the tapioca paste if you want the soup to be slightly thicker

j) Squeeze the lime over the entire soup and leave to simmer for another 5 minutes.

22. Corn and Shrimp Soup

MAKES 8 SERVINGS

INGREDIENTS:

- 2 pounds medium shrimp in shells with heads
- 8 ears corn
- 1 stick butter
- ½ cup all-purpose flour
- 1 large onion, chopped
- 3 green onions, chopped, white and green parts separated
- 1 green bell pepper, chopped
- 2 celery stalks, chopped
- 1 teaspoon minced garlic
- 1 (10-ounce) can original Ro-Tel tomatoes and green chilies
- Salt, freshly ground black pepper, and Creole seasoning, to taste
- ½ pint heavy cream
- 2 tablespoons chopped flat-leaf parsley

INSTRUCTIONS:

a) De-head, peel, and devein the shrimp, placing the heads and shells into a large pot. Set the shrimp aside in the refrigerator.

b) Using a very sharp knife, cut the kernels off the corn cobs into a very large bowl. Using a dull table knife, scrape the cobs to release all of the corn juice into the bowl. Set aside.

c) Add the corn cobs to the pot with the shrimp peelings. Add enough water to cover the shells and cobs and bring to a boil. Reduce the heat to medium and simmer for 30 minutes, uncovered. When slightly cooled, strain the stock into a large measuring cup and discard the shells and cobs. You should have 8 cups of stock; if not, add enough water to make 8 cups of liquid.

d) In a large, heavy pot, melt the butter over medium heat; add the flour and cook, stirring constantly, until the roux turns the color of butterscotch.

e) Add the onion, the white parts of the green onions, the bell pepper, the celery, and the garlic and cook until the onions are translucent. Add the tomatoes and gradually stir in the stock. Season with salt, pepper, and Creole seasoning and simmer, covered, for about 15 minutes. Add the corn and cook 10 minutes longer. Add the shrimp and cook until they are pink, about 2 minutes. Add the cream, green onion tops, and parsley. When ready to serve, heat gently. Do not boil.

23. Clam Chowder

INGREDIENTS

1 Package Cream Soup Base, prepared
0.50 lb. Bacon, small diced
0.75 lb. Onions, small diced
0.50 lb. Celery, small diced
3 lbs. Clams, chopped and Juice (one No. 5 can)
2 lbs. Potatoes, cooked and diced
½ cup Chopped parsley

INSTRUCTIONS:

1.Prepare Cream Soup Base according to package directions.
2.In a separate pot, render bacon until crispy. Add onions and celery and sauté until the onions are translucent.
3.Add the clams in juice, Cream Soup Base and potatoes.
4.Bring to a simmer and simmer 5 minutes.
5.Finish with chopped parsley.

24. Lobster Bisque

INGREDIENTS

5 oz. Vegetable oil
2 lbs. Lobster shells
20 oz. Onions, white, diced
3.75 oz. Tomato paste
3 ¾ Tbsp Paprika
15 oz. Sherry wine
1 ea. Cream Soup Base, 25.22 oz. bag, prepared
1 cup Lobster meat, minced
  As needed Cayenne pepper
  As needed Chive oil

INSTRUCTIONS:

1.In a large stock pot, over medium heat, heat oil and sauté lobster shells for 5 minutes. Add onions, sauté until tender.

2.Add tomato paste and paprika and cook for 3-5 minutes. Add in sherry wine and cook an additional 2-3 minutes.

3.Mix in Cream Soup Base and bring to a simmer. Simmer for 10-15 minutes.

4.Strain through a fine strainer, return to pot. Add minced lobster meat, heat through. Taste and adjust seasoning.
5.Garnish with cayenne pepper and chive oil.

25. Lobster Bisque - Quick Method

INGREDIENTS

- 2.50 oz. Vegetable oil
- 20 oz. Onions, white, diced
- 8.50 oz. Tomato paste
- 5 tsp. Paprika
- 30 oz. Sherry
- 4 Tbsp. Lobster Base
- 1 ea. Cream Soup Base, 25.22 oz. bag, prepared
- 1 cup Lobster meat, minced
- As needed Cayenne pepper
- As needed Chive oil

INSTRUCTIONS:

1.In a large stock pot over low heat, heat oil and sweat onions until tender.

2.Turn heat up to medium, add tomato paste and paprika, cook for 3 minutes. Add sherry wine and lobster base.

3.Add Cream Soup Base and simmer for 5 minutes.

4.Add minced lobster meat, heat through. Taste and adjust seasoning. Garnish with cayenne pepper and chive oil.

26. Louisiana-Style Shrimp and Corn Chowder

INGREDIENTS

20 oz. Bacon, diced fine
30 oz. Celery, diced
30 oz. Onions, diced
0.50 oz. Scallions, chopped
2.50 oz. Garlic, minced
2 #10 can Cream-style corn
2.50 oz. Louisiana Hot Sauce
5 qts. Low Sodium Chicken Base, prepared
5 lbs. Potatoes, russet, peeled, diced
1 ea. Cream Soup Base, 25.22 oz. bag, prepared
2.50 oz. Worcestershire sauce
5 lbs. Shrimp, peeled, deveined
  As needed Kosher salt
  As needed Coarse pepper
  As needed Bacon, crisp

INSTRUCTIONS:

1.In a large stock pot, over medium heat, render bacon until crisp. Add celery, onion and scallions and cook until tender. Add garlic, cook for additional 2 minutes. Add creamed corn, hot sauce and chicken base, bring to simmer. Add potatoes, cook until tender.

2.Add Cream Soup Base and Worcestershire sauce, mix well.
3.Reduce heat to low, add in shrimp, stirring well to combine. Heat through. Taste and adjust seasonings.
4.Garnish with crisp bacon.

27. Pumpkin and Crab Bisque

INGREDIENTS

45 oz. Onion, chopped
2.50 oz. Garlic, minced
6.50 lbs. Lump crabmeat, drained
2 oz. Butter
0.05 oz. Cayenne pepper
0.05 oz. Ginger, ground
3.50 oz. Crab Base
30 oz. Pumpkin purée, canned
1 ea. Cream Soup Base, 25.22 oz. bag, prepared

INSTRUCTIONS:

1.In a food processor, combine onion, garlic, and lump crabmeat.
Pulse until minced well.

2.In a large stock pot over medium heat, melt butter. Add in onion
crab mixture. Allow to sauté for 5-7 minutes. Add cayenne, ginger,
crab base and pumpkin purée; mix well. Add Cream Soup Base,
mix to combine, heat through. Taste and adjust seasoning with salt
and pepper. Reserve warm.

3.To Plate: Serve 5.0 fl. oz. bisque in bowl.

28. Tuna Melt Chowder

INGREDIENTS
0.75 oz. Butter
12.50 oz. Onions, white, chopped
18.75 oz. Potatoes, russet, peeled, diced
1 ea. Cream Soup Base, 25.22 oz. bag, prepared
1.25 lbs. Processed American Cheese Product, cubed
2 lbs. Tuna in oil, drained
As needed Kosher salt
As needed Pepper
As needed Tomato, chopped

INSTRUCTIONS:
1.In a large stock pot, over medium heat, melt butter and sauté onions. Sauté potatoes for 5 minutes. Add Cream Soup Base and cheese to pot. Reduce to low heat, simmer until the potatoes are tender and cheese melted. Add the tuna and cook for an additional 10 minutes. Taste and adjust seasoning.
2.Garnish with tomato.

29. Sweet Corn and Shrimp Chowder

INGREDIENTS

1 Package Cream Soup Base, prepared
1.50 lbs. Shrimp, peeled and deveined
½ cup Lime juice
2 Tbsp. Oil
6 cups Corn kernels, fresh or frozen
1 lb. Bacon, finely chopped
12 oz. Onions, diced
6 oz. Celery, diced
6 oz. Red bell pepper, diced
4 cups Potatoes, red bliss, large diced, par cooked
3 cups Choice Vegetable Base, prepared
  As Needed Kosher salt and cracked pepper
  As Needed Green onion, chopped (optional)

INSTRUCTIONS:

1.Prepare Cream Soup Base according to package directions.

2.Preheat convection oven to 375°F. Combine oil and corn kernels and toss to coat, transfer to parchment-lined sheet pan and roast for 5 to 8 minutes.

3.In a separate pot, render bacon until crisp, remove bacon with slotted spoon, drain and reserve for service.

4.Add onion, celery and red pepper and sauté until onions are translucent.

5.Next, add potatoes and prepared Vegetable Base; bring to boil and simmer until potatoes are tender.

6.Add shrimp and roasted corn and place over medium heat and cook until Chowder reaches 165°F. Hold for service.
7.Season to taste and garnish with chopped green onion and reserved bacon as desired.

30. Tomato Chowder with Shrimp and Dill

INGREDIENTS

1 Package Cream Soup Base, prepared
4 cups Tomato paste
2 ½ cups Ketchup
2.50 qts. Tomato juice
1 qt. Sour cream
3 Tbsp. Caldo de Tomato
½ tsp. Ground thyme
1 ¼ tsp. Garlic powder
½ tsp. Ground ginger
½ cup Fresh chopped dill
1 ¼ tsp. Celery salt
3 ½ cups Cooked baby shrimp to garnish
   As needed Sour cream to garnish
   As nedded Dill sprigs to garnish

INSTRUCTIONS:

1.Combine all ingredients except garnishes. Heat to serving temperature and serve with dollop of sour cream, dill sprig and 1 tablespoon of shrimp.

CHICKEN AND TURKEY

31. Canned Chicken Corn Chowder

Makes: 5-pint jars

INGREDIENTS:
- 3-4 pounds chicken thighs, skinned and boned
- 1 teaspoon salt
- 1 cup onion, diced
- ⅓ cup celery, diced
- 3 cups potatoes, cubed
- 2 cups corn
- 4 cups chicken broth or stock

INSTRUCTIONS:
a) Prepare the pressure canner. Add water into the pressure canner. Insert the trivet and bring it to a boil on medium heat on the stove. Place empty jars into the simmering water for 5-10 minutes. But, do not boil. When done, keep it aside.
b) Dice chicken into cubes and cube vegetables.
c) Add chicken broth or stock into the pot and place over medium heat. Remove from the heat.
d) Place chicken, vegetables, and potatoes into the jars, leaving 1-inch headspace.
e) Sprinkle with salt and hot stock and remove any air bubbles. Place lids.
f) Place jars into the pressure canner and process for 75 minutes.
g) When done, turn off the heat. Wait for 10 minutes.
h) Remove jars from the pressure canner.
i) Let cool overnight.

32. Chicken Chowder Curry

Makes 8 Servings

Ingredients:
- 1 Tablespoon of butter, unsalted
- 2 chopped onions, medium
- 2 teaspoons of curry powder
- 2 chopped ribs of celery
- A dash of cayenne pepper
- 1/4 teaspoons of salt, kosher
- 1/4 teaspoons of pepper, ground
- 5 cups of corn, frozen
- 3 x 14 & 1/2-oz. cans of chicken broth, low sodium
- 1/2 cup of flour, all-purpose
- 1/2 cup of milk, 2%
- 3 cups of chicken breast, cubed and cooked
- 1/3 cup of minced cilantro, fresh

Directions:
a) In large pot, heat the butter on medium heat. Add celery and onions. Stir while cooking till they are tender. Stir in the seasonings and cook for 1/2 minute more.
b) Stir in broth and corn and bring to boil. Reduce the heat and cover pot. Simmer for 15-20 minutes.
c) Whisk milk and flour in small bowl till smooth and stir it into the soup. Bring back to boil. Stir while cooking till thickened, about two minutes. Stir in cilantro and chicken and heat fully through. Serve.

33. Chicken Sausage Chowder with Spinach

Servings 8

Ingredients
1 tablespoon lard, melted
8 ounces chicken sausage, cooked and thinly sliced
1/2 cup scallions, chopped
1 teaspoon ginger garlic paste
1 pound cauliflower, chopped into florets
4 cups vegetable broth
1 pinch red pepper flakes
Kosher salt, to taste
1/2 teaspoon freshly ground black pepper, to taste
1 cup spinach, torn into pieces

Directions
1.Add all ingredients , except for spinach, to your Instant Pot.
2.Secure the lid. Choose the "Manual" setting and cook for 9 minutes under High pressure. Once cooking is complete, use a quick pressure release; carefully remove the lid.
3.Puree the mixture in your food processor.
4.Afterwards, add spinach and seal the lid. Let it stand until the spinach is wilted. Serve in individual bowls. Enjoy!

34. Turkey Chowder with Swiss Chard

Servings 6

Ingredients
1 tablespoon canola oil
1 pound turkey thighs
1 carrot, trimmed and chopped
1 leek, chopped
1 parsnip, chopped
2 garlic cloves, minced
1 ½ quarts turkey broth
2 star anise pods
Sea salt, to taste
1/4 teaspoon ground black pepper, or more to taste
1 bay leaf
1 bunch fresh Thai basil
1/4 teaspoon dried dill
1/2 teaspoon turmeric powder
2 cups Swiss chard, torn into pieces

Directions
1.Press the "Sauté" button and heat the canola oil. Now, brown turkey thighs for 2 to 3 minutes on each side; reserve.
2.Add a splash of turkey broth to scrape up any browned bits from the bottom.
3.Then, add the carrot, leek, parsnip and garlic to the Instant Pot. Sauté until they are softened.
4.Add remaining turkey broth, star anise pods, salt, black pepper, bay leaf, Thai basil, dill, and turmeric powder.
5.Secure the lid. Choose the "Soup" setting and cook for 30 minutes. Once cooking is complete, use a natural pressure release; carefully remove the lid.
6.Stir in Swiss chard while still hot to wilt leaves. Enjoy!

35. Turkey and Daikon Chowder

Serving: 12

Ingredients:
1 lbs Lean Ground Turkey (cooked, drained and crumbled
3 cups Daikon Radish (diced
10 cups Chicken Broth
2 cups Heavy Cream
2 cups Mozzarella (shredded
4 cups Antipasto Trail Mix
1 tbsp. Dried Parsley Leaves
1 tbsp. Dried Chives
1 tsp Salt
1 tsp Ground Black Pepper
1 tsp Garlic Powder

Directions:
1.Place all ingredients in the Instant Pot.
2.Place and lock the lid and manually set the cooking time to 5 minutes at high pressure.
3.When done quick release the pressure.
4.Serve warm.

36. Chicken Bacon Chowder

Serve: 5

 Ingredients:

4 cloves garlic – minced

1 leek – cleaned, trimmed, and sliced

2 ribs celery – diced

1 punnet button mushrooms – sliced

2 medium sweet onion – thinly sliced

4 tbsp butter

2 cups chicken stock

6 boneless, skinless chicken breasts, butterflied

8 oz. cream cheese

1 cup heavy cream

1 packet streaky bacon – cooked crisp, and crumbled

1 tsp salt

1 tsp pepper

1 tsp garlic powder

1 tsp thyme

Directions:

1.Select low setting on your slow cooker.

2.Place 1 cup of chicken stock, onions, garlic, mushroom, leeks, celery, 2 tbsps of butter, and the salt and pepper into your slow cooker.

3.Put the lid on, and cook ingredients on low for 1 hour.

4.Brown chicken breasts in a skillet with 2 tbsp of butter.

5.Add the remaining 1 cup of chicken stock.

6.Scrape the bottom of the skillet to remove any chicken that may have stuck to the bottom.

7.Remove from skillet and set aside, pouring the fat from the pan over the chicken.

8.Add in the thyme, heavy cream, garlic powder and cream cheese into your slow cooker.

9.Stir the contents of the slow cooker until the cream cheese has melted into the dish.

10.Cut the chicken into cubes. Add the bacon and chicken cubes into the slow cooker. Stir **INGREDIENTS**and cook on low for 6-8 hours.

37. <u>Fall Chicken and Root Vegetable Chowder</u>

INGREDIENTS

1 Package Cream Soup Base, prepared
1 lb. Chicken breast, boneless, skinless
¼ cup Lemon juice
4 ea. Garlic cloves, smashed
¼ cup Olive oil
8 oz. Onions, diced
8 oz. Sweet potato, peeled and diced
4 oz. Parsnip, peeled and diced
4 oz. Carrots, peeled and diced
4 oz. Rutabaga, peeled and diced
4 oz. Turnips, peeled and diced
2 ea. Garlic cloves, minced
3 cups Chicken Base, prepared
¼ cup Sage, fresh, chopped
  As needed Kosher salt and cracked pepper
  As needed Baby Arugula, flash-fried (optional)

INSTRUCTIONS:

1.Prepare Cream Soup Base according to package directions.
2.Combine chicken breasts, lemon juice, garlic, and olive oil in a zip top bag and marinate under refrigeration for 1 hour.
3.Preheat convection oven to 375°F. Place drained chicken on parchment-lined sheet pan, season with salt and pepper. Roast for 12 minutes per side or until internal temperature reaches 165°F. Cool and pull chicken.
4.Melt butter in a separate pot. Add onions, sweet potatoes, parsnips, carrots, rutabaga and turnips. Cook until onions are translucent.
5.Add prepared Chicken Base to the vegetable mixture, bring to boil and reduce heat and simmer until vegetables are tender.
6.Add prepared Cream Soup Base, pulled chicken and chopped sage. Place over medium heat and cook until Chowder reaches 165°F. Hold for service.
7.Season to taste and garnish with flash-fried arugula as desired.

38. Chicken Corn Chowder with Smoked Bacon

INGREDIENTS

2.50 oz. Corn oil
5 oz. Smoked bacon, chopped
10 lbs. Chicken thighs, skin on
5 oz. Onions, white, fine diced
2 ½ Tbsp. Garlic, minced
2.50 pts. Chicken Base, prepared
36.875 oz. Cream-style corn
38.125 oz. Corn, canned, drained
1 ea. Cream Soup Base, 25.22 oz. bag, prepared
  As needed Salt
  As needed Pepper
  As needed Chive, minced

INSTRUCTIONS:

1.In a large stock pot over medium heat, heat corn oil and render bacon until brown. Add chicken thighs (skin down) and brown. Add onion and garlic, cook 1 minute. Add the chicken base and let cook over medium heat for 15-20 minutes, or until thighs are very tender.

2.Remove thighs from Chowder, allow to cool enough to handle. Remove skin and shred the meat off the bone, discard skins and bones. Reserve.

3.Next, add the creamed corn and canned corn, stir well. Cook 5 minutes. Whisk in Cream Soup Base and heat through.
4.Add reserved chicken, heat through and serve. Taste and adjust seasoning.
5.Garnish with chive.

39. Del Rio Smoked Chicken Chowder

INGREDIENTS
5 oz. Butter
25 oz. Onion, yellow, diced
25 oz. Celery, diced
10 ea. Arbol chiles, dried, soaked, minced
50 oz. Potatoes, russet, peeled, diced
2.50 qts. Chicken Base, prepared
40 oz. Chicken meat, smoked, pulled
1 ea. Cream Soup Base, 25.22 oz. bag, prepared
  As needed Kosher salt
  As needed Coarse pepper
  As needed Scallions, chopped
  As needed Queso fresco, crumbled

INSTRUCTIONS:

1.In a large stock pot over medium-low heat, melt butter, sweat onions, celery and minced chiles until fragrant and soft.

2.Add potatoes and prepared chicken base. Adjust heat to medium, simmer for 10-15 minutes, or until vegetables are fairly done. Add pulled chicken and Cream Soup Base. Simmer for 15-20 minutes. Taste and adjust seasoning.

3.Garnish with chopped scallions and queso fresco crumbles.

Yield: 10 qts./32 servings (10.0 fl. oz./serving)

40. Fall Festival Turkey Chowder

2.50 oz. Butter
12.50 oz. Onions, white, diced
12.50 oz. Parsnips, peeled, diced
12.50 oz. Turnips, peeled, diced
12.50 oz. Rutabagas, peeled, diced
12.50 oz. Carrots, peeled, diced
12.50 oz. Sweet potatoes, peeled, diced
2.50 qts. Turkey Base
1 ea. Cream Soup Base, 25.22 oz. bag, prepared
40 oz. Turkey breast, roasted, diced
½ cup Sage, fresh, chopped
As needed Kosher salt
As needed Cracked pepper
As needed Cheddar cheese, shredded

INSTRUCTIONS:
1.In a large stock pot over medium heat, melt butter. Sauté onions, parsnips, turnips, rutabagas, carrots and sweet potatoes for 10 minutes.

2.Add turkey base to vegetable mix, bring to a boil, reduce heat and simmer until vegetables are tender, about 20 minutes.

3.Add Cream Soup Base, turkey and sage. Mix to combine, simmer for 30 minutes or until heated through. Taste and adjust seasonings.
4.Garnish with Cheddar cheese.

Yield: 10 qts.; 32 servings (10.0 fl. oz./serving)

41. Loaded White Chicken Chili

INGREDIENTS

1 oz. Vegetable oil
17.20 oz. Onion, diced
4.60 oz. Poblano peppers, diced
0.80 oz. Garlic,minced
2 lbs. Chicken, raw, cubed
0.40 oz. Chili seasoning
2.50 lbs. White beans, canned, drained and rinsed
1 ea. Cream Soup Base, 25.22 oz. bag, prepared

INSTRUCTIONS:

1.In a large stock pot over medium heat, heat oil. Add onion and sauté until translucent. Add poblano peppers and garlic, sauté 2-3 minutes. Add chicken and chili seasoning. Sauté until chicken is cooked. Add white beans and Cream Soup Base and heat through. Taste and adjust seasoning with salt and pepper. Reserve warm.

2.To plate: Serve 10.0 fl. oz. of chili in a bowl. Serve warm.

Serving Suggestion: Serve with flatbread crackers, top with tomato, avocado, crisp crumbled bacon or cheese.

42. <u>Old Fashioned Chicken Pot Pie Chowder</u>

INGREDIENTS

- 5 oz. Butter
- 25 oz. Spanish onion, diced
- 25 oz. Carrots, peeled, large diced
- 25 oz. Celery, large diced
- 5 ea. Potatoes, russet, peeled, large diced
- 5 ea. Sweet potato, large diced
- 25 oz. Parsnips, large diced
- 5 qts. Chicken Base, prepared
- 1 ea. Cream Soup Base, 25.22 oz. bag, prepared
- 5 lbs. Chicken meat, roasted, large diced
- 20 oz. Mushrooms, domestic white, quartered
- 12.50 oz. Green peas, frozen
- 1.25 qts. Heavy cream
- 5 cups Parsley, chopped
- As needed Salt
- As needed Pepper
- As needed Buttermilk dumplings

INSTRUCTIONS:

a) In a large stock pot, over medium heat, melt butter; sweat onions until translucent.

b) Add carrots, celery, both potatoes, and parsnips. Let cook for about 3 minutes. Add chicken base, bring to a rapid boil and reduce heat to low. Let cook for 5 minutes or until vegetables are tender.

c) Add Cream Soup Base and diced chicken meat. Return to medium heat until a light boil. Reduce heat and let simmer for 5 minutes. Add mushrooms and frozen peas; let cook for 5 minutes.

d) Mix in heavy cream and chopped parsley. Taste and adjust seasoning.

e) Garnish with buttermilk dumplings.

43. <u>Creamy Chicken and Corn Chowder</u>

Ingredients:
1 tablespoon olive oil
1 medium onion, diced
2 garlic cloves, minced
2 celery stalks, diced
2 carrots, peeled and diced
4 cups chicken broth
2 cups cooked shredded chicken
2 cups frozen corn
1 cup heavy cream
1 teaspoon dried thyme
Salt and pepper
Instructions:

In a large pot or Dutch oven, heat the olive oil over medium heat.

Add the onion, garlic, celery, and carrots and cook until softened, about 5 minutes.

Add the chicken broth, shredded chicken, frozen corn, thyme, salt, and pepper and bring to a boil.

Reduce the heat and simmer for 15-20 minutes.

Add the heavy cream and stir to combine.

Serve hot.

44. Turkey and Wild Rice Chowder

Ingredients:

1 tablespoon olive oil
1 onion, diced
2 garlic cloves, minced
2 celery stalks, diced
2 carrots, peeled and diced
4 cups chicken broth
2 cups cooked diced turkey
1 cup wild rice, cooked
1 cup heavy cream
1 teaspoon dried thyme
Salt and pepper
Instructions:

In a large pot or Dutch oven, heat the olive oil over medium heat.

Add the onion, garlic, celery, and carrots and cook until softened, about 5 minutes.

Add the chicken broth, diced turkey, wild rice, thyme, salt, and pepper and bring to a boil.

Reduce the heat and simmer for 15-20 minutes.

Add the heavy cream and stir to combine.

Serve hot.

45. Creamy Turkey and Potato Chowder

Ingredients:

1 tablespoon olive oil
1 onion, diced
2 garlic cloves, minced
2 celery stalks, diced
2 carrots, peeled and diced
4 cups chicken broth
2 cups cooked diced turkey
3 cups diced potatoes
1 cup heavy cream
1 teaspoon dried thyme
Salt and pepper
Instructions:

In a large pot or Dutch oven, heat the olive oil over medium heat.

Add the onion, garlic, celery, and carrots and cook until softened, about 5 minutes.

Add the chicken broth, diced turkey, potatoes, thyme, salt, and pepper and bring to a boil.

Reduce the heat and simmer for 15-20 minutes.

Add the heavy cream and stir to combine.

Serve hot.

46. Creamy Chicken and Vegetable Chowder

Ingredients:

1 tablespoon olive oil
1 onion, diced
2 garlic cloves, minced
2 celery stalks, diced
2 carrots, peeled and diced
4 cups chicken broth
2 cups cooked shredded chicken
2 cups mixed frozen vegetables
1 cup heavy cream
1 teaspoon dried thyme
Salt and pepper
Instructions:

In a large pot or Dutch oven, heat the olive oil over medium heat.
Add the onion, garlic, celery, and carrots and cook until softened,
about 5 minutes.
Add the chicken broth, shredded chicken, mixed vegetables,
thyme, salt, and pepper and bring to a boil.
Reduce the heat and simmer for 15-20 minutes

47. Creamy Chicken and Bacon Chowder

Ingredients:
1 tablespoon olive oil
1 onion, diced
2 garlic cloves, minced
2 celery stalks, diced
2 carrots, peeled and diced
4 cups chicken broth
2 cups cooked shredded chicken
1 cup cooked and crumbled bacon
1 cup heavy cream
1 teaspoon dried thyme
Salt and pepper
Instructions:

In a large pot or Dutch oven, heat the olive oil over medium heat.

Add the onion, garlic, celery, and carrots and cook until softened, about 5 minutes.

Add the chicken broth, shredded chicken, crumbled bacon, thyme, salt, and pepper and bring to a boil.

Reduce the heat and simmer for 15-20 minutes.

Add the heavy cream and stir to combine.

Serve hot.

48. Creamy Chicken and Mushroom Chowder

Ingredients:

1 tablespoon olive oil
1 onion, diced
2 garlic cloves, minced
2 celery stalks, diced
2 carrots, peeled and diced
4 cups chicken broth
2 cups cooked shredded chicken
2 cups sliced mushrooms
1 cup heavy cream
1 teaspoon dried thyme
Salt and pepper
Instructions:

In a large pot or Dutch oven, heat the olive oil over medium heat.

Add the onion, garlic, celery, and carrots and cook until softened, about 5 minutes.

Add the chicken broth, shredded chicken, sliced mushrooms, thyme, salt, and pepper and bring to a boil.

Reduce the heat and simmer for 15-20 minutes.

Add the heavy cream and stir to combine.

Serve hot.

49. Creamy Chicken and Spinach Chowder

Ingredients:

1 tablespoon olive oil
1 onion, diced
2 garlic cloves, minced
2 celery stalks, diced
2 carrots, peeled and diced
4 cups chicken broth
2 cups cooked shredded chicken
2 cups packed baby spinach leaves
1 cup heavy cream
1 teaspoon dried thyme
Salt and pepper
Instructions:

In a large pot or Dutch oven, heat the olive oil over medium heat.

Add the onion, garlic, celery, and carrots and cook until softened, about 5 minutes.

Add the chicken broth, shredded chicken, baby spinach leaves, thyme, salt, and pepper and bring to a boil.

Reduce the heat and simmer for 15-20 minutes.

Add the heavy cream and stir to combine.

Serve hot.

50. Creamy Chicken and Sweet Potato Chowder

Ingredients:

1 tablespoon olive oil
1 onion, diced
2 garlic cloves, minced
2 celery stalks, diced
2 carrots, peeled and diced
4 cups chicken broth
2 cups cooked shredded chicken
2 cups diced sweet potatoes
1 cup heavy cream
1 teaspoon dried thyme
Salt and pepper
Instructions:

In a large pot or Dutch oven, heat the olive oil over medium heat.
Add the onion, garlic, celery, and carrots and cook until softened, about 5 minutes.
Add the chicken broth, shredded chicken, sweet potatoes, thyme, salt, and pepper and bring to a boil.
Reduce the heat and simmer for 15-20 minutes.
Add the heavy cream and stir to combine.
6. Serve hot.

51. Creamy Chicken and Leek Chowder

Ingredients:

1 tablespoon olive oil
1 onion, diced
2 garlic cloves, minced
2 celery stalks, diced
2 leeks, cleaned and sliced
4 cups chicken broth
2 cups cooked shredded chicken
1 cup heavy cream
1 teaspoon dried thyme
Salt and pepper
Instructions:

In a large pot or Dutch oven, heat the olive oil over medium heat.
Add the onion, garlic, celery, and leeks and cook until softened, about 5 minutes.
Add the chicken broth, shredded chicken, thyme, salt, and pepper and bring to a boil.
Reduce the heat and simmer for 15-20 minutes.
Add the heavy cream and stir to combine.
Serve hot.

VEGETABLE

52. Lotsa Vegetable Chowder

SERVES 4 TO 6

8 small Yukon Gold, white, or russet potatoes (about 2 pounds), cut into ½-inch chunks
½ small onion, peeled and chopped
3 ears fresh corn, kernels removed (about 1¾ cups), cobs reserved
2 medium carrots, peeled and diced
2 stalks of celery, chopped
¼ cup chopped red bell pepper
1 cup chopped broccoli and cauliflower stalks, outer fibrous parts removed and discarded (about ½ pound)
1 clove garlic, peeled and minced
2 tablespoons chopped thyme
⅛ teaspoon white pepper
2 teaspoons ground cumin
3 tablespoons chopped dill
Salt to taste

1. In a large pot, combine the potatoes, onion, corn kernels and cobs, carrots, celery, pepper, broccoli and cauliflower, garlic, thyme, white pepper, cumin, and 6 cups water. Bring to a boil over high heat. Reduce the heat to medium-low and simmer for 30 minutes, or until the vegetables are tender.
2. Remove the corn cobs and let cool. Remove 1 cup of the soup and puree in a blender with a tight-fitting lid, covered with a towel. (If you like a thicker soup, puree 2 cups.) Return the pureed soup to the pot and add the dill. Scrape corn cobs with back of a knife to remove the creamy corn bits from the kernel, and add the bits to the pot. Stir well and season with salt.

53. Fat-Free Cauliflower-Crab Chowder

SERVES: 2

INGREDIENTS
cups chopped cauliflower
cups nonfat chicken broth
cup diced red pepper
cup diced celery
cup chopped celery
1 ½ cups fat-free half and half
tablespoons flour
ounces cooked crabmeat
1 tablespoon ± old bay seasoning (to taste)

DIRECTIONS
1In a large sauce pan combine chicken broth and cauliflower and bring to a boil. Boil for 5 minutes then adds bell pepper, celery, and onion.
2Return to a boil and simmer for 15 minutes.
3Stir together half and half and flour until smooth.
4Add to cauliflower mixture and cook (stirring frequently) for 5 to 10 minutes.
5Add crab and old bay.

54. Fall Harvest Vegetable Chowder

SERVES 6

1 medium yellow onion, peeled and diced (about 1 cup)
3 celery stalks, diced (about 1 cup)
2 medium carrots, peeled and diced (about 1 cup)
6 cups Vegetable Stock, or low-sodium vegetable broth
2 small zucchini, diced
2 small yams, peeled and diced
4 bay leaves
2 tablespoons thyme
3 to 4 ears corn, kernels removed (about 2 cups)
4 cups packed spinach leaves

1. Place the onion, celery, carrots, and ½ cup vegetable stock in a large soup pot and sauté over medium-high heat for 6 to 8 minutes, or until the onion is translucent.
2. Add the zucchini, yams, bay leaves, thyme, and remaining broth and bring to a boil over high heat. Reduce the heat to medium-low and simmer for 20 to 30 minutes, or until the vegetables are tender.
3. Add half the corn and cook for 10 to 15 more minutes. Remove the bay leaves.
4. Puree the soup using an immersion blender or in batches in a blender with a tight-fitting lid, covered with a towel. Return the soup to the pot and add the remaining corn and spinach leaves. Cook for 5 more minutes, or until the spinach is wilted. Stir well and serve hot.

55. Winter Vegetable and Ham Chowder

Serving: 5 servings

Ingredients
3 medium potatoes, peeled and cut into 1/4-inch pieces
1/2 cup chopped onion
1 cup water
3/4 teaspoon onion salt or onion powder
1/2 teaspoon pepper
1/8 teaspoon salt
2 drops Louisiana-style hot sauce
1/2 cup cubed fully cooked ham (1/4-inch pieces)
1 cup fresh or frozen brussels sprouts, quartered
1-1/2 cups milk
3/4 cup shredded Colby-Monterey Jack cheese, divided

Direction
Boil water with the potatoes, and onion in a large saucepan.
Lower the heat, then cover with a lid. Let it cook until it softens
for 10 to 12 minutes. With the water, mash the potatoes
(mixture won't be smooth) and add in the pepper, onion salt,
hot sauce, and salt. Let it rest.
Sauté the brussels sprouts with the ham in a large nonstick
skillet spread with cooking spray, for 5-6 minutes until the
sprouts soften. Mix in the potato mixture, then pour the milk in.
Let it boil, then lower the heat. Leave it uncovered while
simmering until thoroughly heated. Stir while cooking for 5 to 6
minutes.
Gently add in the half cup of cheese, and let it melt for 2 to 3
minutes. Top with the leftover cheese.

56. <u>Oyster mushroom chowder</u>

Makes: 6 Servings

INGREDIENTS:
- 1 quart Oysters
- 1 cup Oyster liquor
- 3 tablespoons Butter
- 1 tablespoon Flour
- 1 cup Milk
- ½ cup Cream
- 2 tablespoons Shallots, minced
- Salt and pepper
- ½ pounds Mushrooms
- 2 teaspoons Parsley, minced

INSTRUCTIONS:
a) Heat oysters in liquor over low heat until edges curl. Drain, saving liquor.

b) Melt 1 tablespoon butter, blend in flour, add milk gradually, stirring constantly. Bring to boiling and cook 1 minute.

c) Add cream, shallots, parsley, salt and pepper. Warm mushrooms in remaining butter until heated but not brown.

d) Combine mushrooms, oysters, and oyster liquor to cream sauce. Serve immediately.

57. <u>Cauliflower and Cheese Chowder</u>

Ingredients:
4 cups cauliflower florets, chopped
4 bacon strips
1 tbsp organic butter
2 cloves of garlic, minced
1 onion, chopped fine
¼ cup almond flour
4 cups low-sodium chicken broth
½ cup milk
¼ cup light cream
1 cup cheddar, shredded
Salt and pepper to taste

Directions:
1.Cook the bacon in a large pot. Remove from the pot when cooked and set aside.
2.Using the same pot set the heat on medium and throws in the onions. Cook for 3 minutes and then add the garlic and cauliflower florets and cook for another 5 minutes.
3.Add the flour into the pot and continuously whisk for a minute.
4.Pour the chicken broth, milk, and light cream and stir for 3 minutes.
5.Allow to simmer for 15 minutes and then turn off the heat.
6.Add the cheddar cheese into the pot, season with salt and pepper and stir again.
7.Serve with the chopped bacon on top.

58. Leek Soup

MAKES 4

INGREDIENTS:
- 2 tablespoons butter
- 3 cups leeks, sliced
- 1 ½ cups onions, sliced
- 2 tablespoons flour
- 6 cups chicken broth
- 1 ½ teaspoon salt or to taste
- ½ teaspoon ground white pepper

INSTRUCTIONS:
a) Melt butter in a saucepan over moderate heat
b) Stir in leek and onion pieces to coat with butter
c) Cover the pan and reduce the heat
d) Cook slowly, stirring occasionally for 10 to 15 minutes until vegetables are very soft, but not colored
e) Uncover and sprinkle the flour on the leeks and onions Stir to distribute the flour
f) Cook for 2 minutes on moderate heat
g) Remove from heat and let cook a moment
h) Stirring continually, add 2 cups of broth
i) Bring to a simmer
j) When liquid is smooth and starts to thicken, stir in the remainder of the broth.
k) Heat soup to a boil, cover the pan and lower the heat
l) Simmer for about 20 minutes.
m) To serve, mash, blend or purée the soup to desired consistency Serve warm

59. Jamaican Squash Soup

MAKES 4

INGREDIENTS:
- 1 large onion, peeled and chopped
- 1 carrot, peeled and chopped
- 1 jalapeño, pepper, seeds removed, finely chopped
- 3 tablespoons butter
- 2 teaspoon ground cumin
- 2 teaspoon ground coriander
- ½ teaspoon ground cinnamon
- ½ teaspoon cayenne pepper
- ½ teaspoon chili powder
- 1 large spaghetti squash, peeled and diced
- Chicken stock to cover vegetables, about 3 cups
- Juice of 1 orange
- Juice of 1 lime

ANCHO CREAM
- 2 to 3 Ancho chilies, halved, stemmed, and seeded
- 6 tablespoons almond milk
- 4 tablespoons sour cream
- Salt
- Pepper
- Lime juice to taste

INSTRUCTIONS:

a) In a large heavy pot, sweat onion, carrot, and Jalapeno pepper in butter until soft

b) Add cumin, coriander, cinnamon, cayenne, and chili powder

c) Cook for additional 2 minutes over low heat

d) Add squash

e) Cover mixture with stock, juice of one orange, and juice of a lime Simmer until squash is soft, about ½ hour

f) Allow cooling

g) Purée mixture in processor or use immersion blender

h) Return soup to the pan, season with salt and pepper

i) Reheat and adjust seasoning if necessary

j) Swirl in Ancho Cream

k) Garnish with sour cream thinned with some heavy cream

l) Place dab in the center of a soup bowl and using a toothpick, drag from center to outside and form a star or spider web

60. Classic Cream of Tomato Chowder

INGREDIENTS

1 Package Cream Soup Base, prepared
4 cups Tomato paste
2 ½ cups Ketchup
2.50 qts. Tomato juice
3 Tbsp. Caldo de Tomato
½ tsp. Ground thyme
1 ¼ tsp. Garlic powder
½ tsp. Ground ginger
1 ¼ tsp. Celery salt

INSTRUCTIONS:
1. Combine all ingredients and heat to serving temperature.
2. Serve with croutons and chopped parsley.

61. Cream of Spinach Chowder

INGREDIENTS

1 Package Cream Soup Base, prepared
1 Onion
16 oz. Spinach, chopped (or 2 packages, frozen, thawed)
1 Tbsp. 095™ Chicken Base

INSTRUCTIONS:
1.Prepare Cream Soup Base according to package directions.
2.In a separate pan, sauté onions until tender. Add spinach and sauté until warm.
3.Add spinach mixture into Chowder.
4.Add chicken base.
5.Simmer lightly until service.

62. Cream of Potato Chowder

INGREDIENTS

30 oz. Butter, divided
20 oz. Onions, chopped
5 ea. Bay leaves, whole
½ tsp. Thyme, ground
10 lbs. Potatoes, russet, peeled, sliced
3.75 qts. Chicken Base, prepared
1 ea. Cream Soup Base, 25.22 oz. bag, prepared
½ tsp. White pepper, ground
  As needed Salt
  As needed Cheddar cheese, shredded

INSTRUCTIONS:

1.In a large stock pot, melt 10.0 oz of butter and sweat onions. Add bay leaves, thyme, potatoes and chicken base, cook until potatoes are fork tender. Remove bay leaves.

2.In a food processor, in batches, purée until smooth and add Cream Soup Base, finish with remaining butter and white pepper. Taste and adjust seasoning.

3.Garnish with Cheddar cheese.

63. Cream of Roasted Red Pepper and Tomato Chowder

NGREDIENTS

5 oz. Vegetable oil
12.50 oz. Onions, white, diced
0.75 oz. Garlic, minced
2.50 qts. Roasted red pepper, chopped
2.50 qts. Tomatoes, diced, canned, not drained
7.50 oz. Pesto
1 ea. Cream Soup Base, 25.22 oz. bag, prepared
2 lbs. Parmesan, shredded
  As needed Basil, chiffonade

INSTRUCTIONS:

1.In a large stock pot over medium heat, sauté onions until translucent; add garlic, sauté 1 minute.
2.Add peppers and tomatoes, bring to simmer. Add pesto and mix well.

3.In a food processor, in batches, purée mixture until smooth. Return to pan over medium heat. Add Cream Soup Base and heat through. Taste and adjust seasoning.

4.Garnish with 1 oz. Parmesan and basil chiffonade.

Yield: 10 qts.; 32 servings (10.0 fl. oz./serving)

64. Gingered Carrot Chowder

INGREDIENTS

5 oz. Vegetable oil
40 oz. Onions, white, cut into 1" pieces
5 tsp. Ginger, ground
2 ½ tsp. Salt
2 ½ tsp. Cumin, ground
2 ½ tsp. Dry mustard
1 ¼ tsp. Mace, ground
1 ¼ tsp. Cinnamon, ground
1 ¼ tsp. Black pepper
¾ tsp. Red pepper, ground
150 oz. Carrots, peeled, cubed
5 qts. Concentrated Chicken Flavor Base, prepared
1 ea. Cream Soup Base, 25.22 oz. bag, prepared
40 oz. Milk, skim
   As needed Nutmeg, fresh grated

INSTRUCTIONS:

1.In a large stock pot, over medium heat, heat oil. Add onions and spices, sauté for 2 minutes. Reduce heat to low, cover and cook 5 minutes or until tender.

2.Add carrots and chicken flavor base. Increase heat, bring to boil, reduce heat and simmer, partially covered for 30 minutes or until carrots are soft.

3.Using a blender, in batches, purée carrot-onion mixture, process until smooth. Return purée to pan over medium heat, stir in Cream Soup Base and milk. Heat through. Taste and adjust seasoning.
4.Garnish with nutmeg.

65. Rustic Italian Tomato Chowder with Spinach

INGREDIENTS

1 Package Cream Soup Base, prepared
2 oz. Olive oil
2 Onions, chopped
4 Garlic cloves, chopped
20 oz. Fresh spinach, chopped
2 ½ cups Tomato paste
2.50 qts. Frutta di Orto marinara sauce
4 15 oz. cans Diced tomatoes with juice
¼ cup Fresh chopped basil
1 Tbsp. Fresh thyme sprigs
5 cups Tomato sauce

INSTRUCTIONS:

1.Sauté onions and garlic in oil until translucent. Add Spinach and sauté until wilted.
2.Add remaining ingredients and heat to serving temperature. Garnish with a mini bruchetta.

66. Spicy Roasted Tomato and Garlic Chowder

INGREDIENTS

1 Package Cream Soup Base, prepared
12 lbs. Roma tomatoes
1 cup Olive oil
5 cups Caldo de Tomate, prepared
1 ¼ cups Salsa Roja
4 cups Tomato paste
1 head Garlic, roasted
1 ¼ cups Cilantro, chopped
½ cups Lime juice, fresh
3 ½ cups Queso Fresco, crumbled
  As needed Cilantro springs
  As needed Lime wedges

INSTRUCTIONS:

1.Coat tomatoes with oil and roast until skin begins to blacken. Purée in blender with caldo until smooth.

2.Combine with Cream Soup Base, salsa roja, tomato paste, and garlic. Heat to serving temperature.

3.Finish with cilantro and lime juice. Garnish with cheese and cilantro sprigs with a lime wedge on the side.

CORN

67. Harvest Corn Chowder

Serving: about 12 servings

Ingredients
- 1 medium onion, chopped
- 1 tablespoon butter
- 2 cans (14-3/4 ounces each) cream-style corn
- 4 cups whole kernel corn
- 4 cups diced peeled potatoes
- 1 can (10-3/4 ounces) condensed cream of mushroom soup, undiluted
- 1 jar (6 ounces) sliced mushrooms, drained
- 3 cups milk
- 1/2 medium green pepper, chopped
- 1/2 to 1 medium sweet red pepper, chopped
- Pepper to taste
- 1/2 pound bacon, cooked and crumbled

Direction
a) Saut é onion with butter until tender in a large pot.
b) Pour in soup, cream-style corn, kernel corn, potatoes, and mushroom. Then add in milk, red and green peppers, and season with pepper.
c) After bringing to boil, lower heat and simmer (covered) until vegetables are tender or about 30 minutes. Sprinkle with bacon.

68. <u>Zippy Chicken And Corn Chowder</u>

Serving: 8 servings

Ingredients
- 1/4 cup butter
- 1 large onion, chopped
- 1 medium green pepper, chopped
- 1/4 cup all-purpose flour
- 1 tablespoon paprika
- 2 medium potatoes, peeled and chopped
- 1 carton (32 ounces) chicken broth
- 1 skinned rotisserie chicken, shredded
- 6 cups fresh or frozen corn
- 1 tablespoon Worcestershire sauce
- 1/2 to 1 teaspoon hot pepper sauce
- 1 teaspoon salt
- 1 cup 2% milk

Direction
a) Heat butter in a stockpot on moderately high heat. Put in pepper and onion, then cook for 3 to 4 minutes while stirring, until the vegetables are tender-crisp. Stir in paprika and flour until combined.
b) Put in potatoes, then stir in broth. Bing the mixture to a boil. Lower heat and simmer with a cover for 12 to 15 minutes, until softened.
c) Stir in salt, sauces, corn and chicken, then bring to a boil. Lower heat and cook without a cover for 4 to 6 minutes, until corn is softened. Put in milk and heat through without boiling.

69. Corn Chowder

Makes: 4 Servings

INGREDIENTS
- 1 teaspoon garlic
- ½ teaspoon dried thyme
- ½ teaspoon sea salt
- 4 cups corn kernels (from 4 ears of corn)
- ¼ cup extra-virgin olive oil
- 2 cups water
- 1 recipe Coconut Bacon , diced
- 1 recipe Jalapeño-Lime Cream

INSTRUCTIONS
a) Place the garlic, thyme, and salt in a food processor, and process into small pieces. Add the corn, oil, and water and process into a chunky chowder.
b) Divide among four serving bowls. Top each portion with diced Coconut Bacon and a dollop of Jalapeño-Lime Cream, and serve immediately.

70. New England Chicken 'n' Corn Chowder

Makes: 4-6

INGREDIENTS:
- ¼ pound bacon or salt pork, diced
- 1 cup chopped onion
- ½ cup chopped celery
- 4 cups chicken broth
- 2 cups peeled potatoes, cut in ½-inch cubes
- 10 ounces frozen corn or kernels from 2 ears of corn
- 1 teaspoon salt or to taste
- ⅛ teaspoon ground pepper
- 2 cups cooked, diced chicken
- 1 cup (½-pint) heavy cream Oyster crackers, for garnish

INSTRUCTIONS:
a) In large saucepan over medium-high heat, sauté bacon for 3 minutes until its fat has been rendered.
b) Add onions and celery and cook 3 minutes longer. Stir in broth and bring to a boil, whisking constantly.
c) Add potatoes and corn, season with salt and pepper and cook 5 to 10 minutes or until tender. Stir in chicken and cream, simmer 3 minutes and serve with oyster crackers.

71. Cherry Tomato and Corn Chowder

SERVES 4

- 1 tablespoon olive oil
- 1 medium onion, diced
- 2 stalks celery, diced
- 2 garlic cloves, minced
- 1 pint small cherry tomatoes, halved
- 2½ cups frozen corn kernels, thawed
- 2 cups low-fat milk
- 1 teaspoon chopped fresh thyme
- ¼ teaspoon freshly ground pepper
- 1 cup low-sodium vegetable or chicken broth
- 3 green onions, thinly sliced, for garnish
- 2 slices turkey bacon, cooked and crumbled, for garnish (optional)

1. Heat the oil in a large stockpot over medium-high heat. Add the onion, celery, and garlic and cook, stirring, until the onion is soft, about 5 minutes.

2. Add the tomatoes and cook for another 2 to 3 minutes, until the tomatoes just begin to break down.

3. Place 1½ cups of the corn, 1 cup of the milk, the thyme, and the pepper in a blender or food processor and process until smooth.

4. Transfer the pureed mixture to the stockpot and bring to a simmer.

5. Add the remaining 1 cup of corn and 1 cup of milk to the pot along with the broth. Stir well and cook over medium heat for about 5 minutes until heated through.

6. Serve hot, garnished with the green onions and bacon.

72. Quinoa corn chowder

Yield: 1 Servings
Ingredient

- ½ cup Quinoa, cooked
- 1 cup Potato, cubed
- 2 Carrots
- 2 smalls Onions
- 3 cups Corn -- can be part creamed
- 2 cups Milk
- 1½ teaspoon Salt
- Fresh ground black pepper
- ½ cup Parsley
- Butter

Simmer quinoa, potato, carrot, celery onion until tender (About 15 min).

Add corn. Bring back to boil and simmer another 5 minutes or so. Add Milk.

Bring jujst to boil. Season to taste. Garnish with parsley and dab of butter.

73. Corn And Potato Chowder

Makes 4 to 6 servings

- 1 tablespoon olive oil
- 1 medium onion, chopped
- 1 celery rib, chopped
- 3 medium Yukon Gold potatoes, peeled and diced
- 4 cups vegetable broth, homemade
- Salt and freshly ground black pepper
- 3 cups fresh, frozen, or canned corn kernels
- 1 cup plain unsweetened soy milk
- 1 tablespoon minced green onions or chives, for garnish

a) In large soup pot, heat the oil over medium heat. Add the onion and celery. Cover and cook until the vegetables are softened, about 10 minutes.
b) Add the potatoes, broth, and salt and pepper to taste. Bring to a boil, then reduce heat to low and simmer, uncovered, until the potatoes begin to soften, about 30 minutes.
c) Add the corn and simmer 15 minutes longer. Puree about half the soup in the pot with an immersion blender or in a blender or food processor, and return to the pot. Stir in the soy milk and taste, adjusting seasonings if necessary.
d) Ladle the soup into bowls, garnish with green onions, and serve.

74. Roasted Corn Chowder

Ingredients:

4 ears of corn, husks removed
1 onion, diced
2 garlic cloves, minced
2 celery stalks, diced
4 cups chicken broth
1 cup diced potatoes
1 cup heavy cream
Salt and pepper
Olive oil
Instructions:

Preheat the oven to 400°F (200°C).

Brush the ears of corn with olive oil and place them on a baking sheet.

Roast the corn for 15-20 minutes, or until lightly browned.

Remove the corn from the oven and let it cool slightly.

Cut the kernels off the cobs and set aside.

In a large pot or Dutch oven, heat some olive oil over medium heat.

Add the onion, garlic, and celery and cook until softened, about 5 minutes.

Add the chicken broth, roasted corn kernels, and potatoes and bring to a boil.

Reduce the heat and simmer for 15-20 minutes, or until the potatoes are tender.

Add the heavy cream and stir to combine.

Serve hot.

75. <u>Smoky Corn Chowder</u>

Ingredients:

4 slices bacon, chopped
1 onion, diced
2 garlic cloves, minced
2 celery stalks, diced
4 cups chicken broth
3 cups fresh or frozen corn kernels
1 cup diced potatoes
1 cup heavy cream
1 teaspoon smoked paprika
Salt and pepper
Instructions:

In a large pot or Dutch oven, cook the chopped bacon until crispy.

Remove the bacon with a slotted spoon and set aside.

Add the onion, garlic, and celery to the bacon fat and cook until softened, about 5 minutes.

Add the chicken broth, corn kernels, and potatoes and bring to a boil.

Reduce the heat and simmer for 15-20 minutes, or until the potatoes are tender.

Add the heavy cream, smoked paprika, and stir to combine.

Serve hot, topped with the crispy bacon.

76. Spicy Corn Chowder

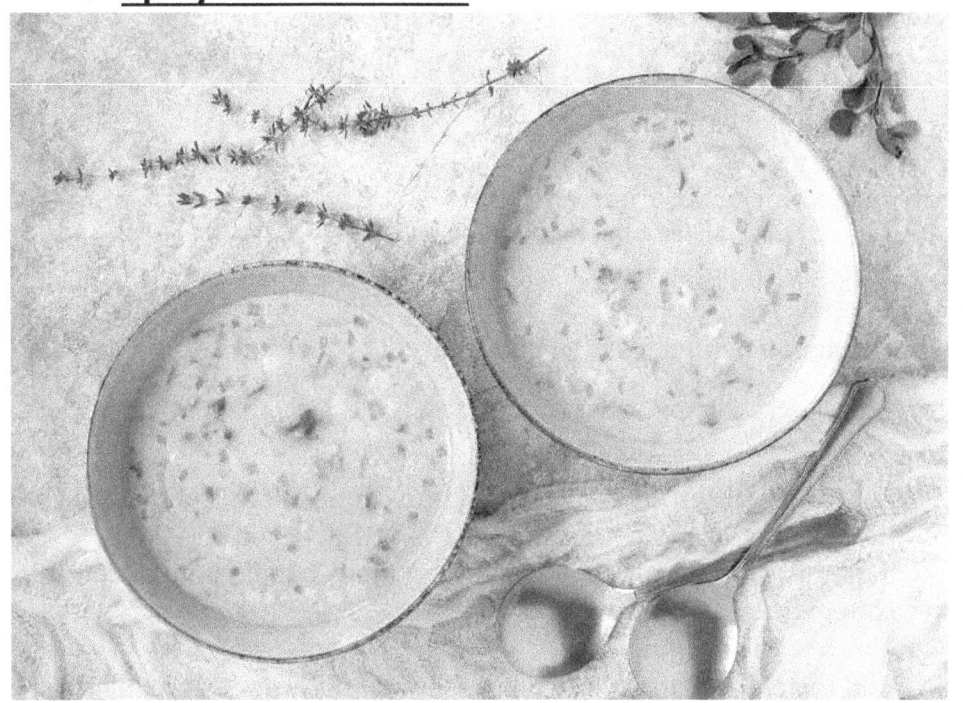

Ingredients:

4 slices bacon, chopped
1 onion, diced
2 garlic cloves, minced
2 celery stalks, diced
4 cups chicken broth
3 cups fresh or frozen corn kernels
1 cup diced potatoes
1 cup heavy cream
1 jalapeno pepper, seeded and minced
Salt and pepper
Instructions:

In a large pot or Dutch oven, cook the chopped bacon until crispy. Remove the bacon with a slotted spoon and set aside.
3. Add the onion, garlic, and celery to the bacon fat and cook until softened, about 5 minutes.

Add the chicken broth, corn kernels, and potatoes and bring to a boil.

Reduce the heat and simmer for 15-20 minutes, or until the potatoes are tender.

Add the heavy cream and jalapeno pepper and stir to combine.

Serve hot, seasoned with salt and pepper to taste.

77. Vegan Corn Chowder

Ingredients:

1 onion, diced
2 garlic cloves, minced
2 celery stalks, diced
4 cups vegetable broth
3 cups fresh or frozen corn kernels
1 cup diced potatoes
1 cup unsweetened almond milk
1 tablespoon nutritional yeast
Salt and pepper
Olive oil
Instructions:

In a large pot or Dutch oven, heat some olive oil over medium heat.

Add the onion, garlic, and celery and cook until softened, about 5 minutes.

Add the vegetable broth, corn kernels, and potatoes and bring to a boil.

Reduce the heat and simmer for 15-20 minutes, or until the potatoes are tender.

Use an immersion blender or transfer the soup to a blender and puree until smooth.

Return the soup to the pot and stir in the almond milk and nutritional yeast.

Serve hot, seasoned with salt and pepper to taste.

78. Creamy Corn and Potato Chowder

Ingredients:

4 slices bacon, chopped
1 onion, diced
2 garlic cloves, minced
2 celery stalks, diced
4 cups chicken broth
3 cups fresh or frozen corn kernels
1 cup diced potatoes
1 cup heavy cream
1 tablespoon flour
Salt and pepper
Instructions:

In a large pot or Dutch oven, cook the chopped bacon until crispy.

Remove the bacon with a slotted spoon and set aside.

Add the onion, garlic, and celery to the bacon fat and cook until softened, about 5 minutes.

Add the chicken broth, corn kernels, and potatoes and bring to a boil.

Reduce the heat and simmer for 15-20 minutes, or until the potatoes are tender.

In a small bowl, whisk together the heavy cream and flour.

Add the cream mixture to the soup and stir to combine.

Serve hot, topped with the crispy bacon and seasoned with salt and pepper to taste.

79. <u>Southwestern Corn Chowder</u>

Ingredients:

4 slices bacon, chopped
1 onion, diced
2 garlic cloves, minced
2 celery stalks, diced
4 cups chicken broth
3 cups fresh or frozen corn kernels
1 cup diced potatoes
1 cup heavy cream
1 teaspoon cumin
1 teaspoon chili powder
Salt and pepper
Instructions:

In a large pot or Dutch oven, cook the chopped bacon until crispy.
Remove the bacon with a slotted spoon and set aside.
Add the onion, garlic, and celery to the bacon fat and cook until softened, about 5 minutes.
Add the chicken broth, corn kernels, and potatoes and bring to a boil.
Reduce the heat and simmer for 15-20 minutes, or until the potatoes are tender.
Add the heavy cream, cumin, chili powder, and stir to combine.
Serve hot, topped with the crispy bacon and seasoned with salt and pepper to taste

80. Smoky Corn and Bacon Chowder

Ingredients:
4 slices bacon, chopped
1 onion, diced
2 garlic cloves, minced
2 celery stalks, diced
4 cups chicken broth
3 cups fresh or frozen corn kernels
1 cup diced potatoes
1 cup heavy cream
1 teaspoon smoked paprika
Salt and pepper
Instructions:

In a large pot or Dutch oven, cook the chopped bacon until crispy.

Remove the bacon with a slotted spoon and set aside.

Add the onion, garlic, and celery to the bacon fat and cook until softened, about 5 minutes.

Add the chicken broth, corn kernels, and potatoes and bring to a boil.

Reduce the heat and simmer for 15-20 minutes, or until the potatoes are tender.

Add the heavy cream and smoked paprika and stir to combine.

Serve hot, topped with the crispy bacon and seasoned with salt and pepper to taste.

81. Slow Cooker Corn Chowder

Ingredients:

6 cups fresh or frozen corn kernels
1 onion, diced
2 garlic cloves, minced
3 cups chicken broth
1 cup diced potatoes
1 cup heavy cream
Salt and pepper
Instructions:

In a slow cooker, combine the corn kernels, onion, garlic, chicken broth, and potatoes.

Cover and cook on low for 6-8 hours, or on high for 3-4 hours, until the potatoes are tender.

Use an immersion blender or transfer the soup to a blender and puree until smooth.

Return the soup to the slow cooker and stir in the heavy cream.

Season with salt and pepper to taste and serve hot.

82. Roasted Corn Chowder with Bacon

Ingredients:

6 ears of corn, shucked and kernels removed
1 onion, diced
2 garlic cloves, minced
4 cups chicken broth
1 cup diced potatoes
1 cup heavy cream
4 slices bacon, chopped
Salt and pepper
Olive oil
Instructions:

Preheat the oven to 400°F.
Spread the corn kernels on a baking sheet and drizzle with some olive oil. Toss to coat.
Roast the corn in the oven for 20-25 minutes, or until lightly browned.
In a large pot or Dutch oven, cook the chopped bacon until crispy. Remove the bacon with a slotted spoon and set aside.
Add the onion and garlic to the bacon fat and cook until softened, about 5 minutes.
Add the chicken broth, roasted corn, and potatoes and bring to a boil.
Reduce the heat and simmer for 15-20 minutes, or until the potatoes are tender.
Use an immersion blender or transfer the soup to a blender and puree until smooth.
Return the soup to the pot and stir in the heavy cream.
Serve hot, topped with the crispy bacon and seasoned with salt and pepper to taste.

BEEF AND PORK

83. Corned Beef Chowder

Serves 6-8.

3 cups milk
- 1 10 oz can cream of celery soup
- 1 10 oz can cream of potato soup
- 1 12 oz can corned beef
- 1 10 oz pkg frozen broccoli (or fresh)
- 1 small onion, chopped

a) In large dutch oven mix all ingredients except corned beef.
   Bring to a simmer, stirring to prevent scalding.
b) Reduce heat and simmer until broccoli and onion are tender.
c) Add beef and simmer until beef is warmed.

84. <u>Meat ball chowder</u>

Ingredient
- 2 pounds Ground lean beef
- 2 tablespoons Milk
- Spices

a) To make meatballs combine all ingredients except oil; mix thoroughly. Form into balls about the size of walnuts (40-50 balls). Heat oil and brown balls lightly.

b) Chowder: In a 8-10 quart kettle bring all ingredients except Mexicorn to a boil. Reduce heat and simmer 30 minutes, adding Mexicorn for last 10 minutes. Add browned meat balls. Makes 6-7 quarts.

85. Sausage Bacon and Mushroom Chowder

Serving: 14

Ingredients:
4 cups Chicken Broth
2 cups Heavy Cream
2 cups Mushrooms (sliced
2 cups Ground Sausage (cooked
6 rashers Bacon (fried and crumbled
1 cup Daikon Radish (diced
½ cup Onion (diced
½ cup Red Bell Pepper (diced
½ cup Parmesan Cheese
1 tbsp. Dried Parsley Leaves
1 tsp Garlic Powder
1 tsp Salt
1 tsp Ground Black Pepper
½ tsp Thyme

Directions:
1.Place all ingredients in the Instant Pot.
2.Place and lock the lid and manually set the cooking time to 5 minutes at high pressure.
3.When done quick release the pressure.
4.Serve warm.

86. Chipped Beef Chowder

INGREDIENTS

1.25 oz. Butter
12.50 oz. Onions, white, diced
12.50 oz. Carrots, peeled, diced
25 oz. Potatoes, russet, peeled, diced
12.50 oz. Corn, white
1 lbs. Dried beef, diced
1.25 qts. Low Sodium Chicken Base, prepared
1 ea. Cream Soup Base, 25.22 oz. bag, prepared
1 ½ Tbsp. White pepper, ground
  As needed Parsley, minced

INSTRUCTIONS:

1.In a large stock pot, over medium heat, melt butter and sauté onions and carrots until tender.

2.Add the potatoes, corn, beef and chicken base. Simmer until the potatoes are tender. Add Cream Soup Base and simmer for 5 minutes. Taste and adjust seasoning.

3.Garnish with parsley.

87. Corned Beef and Cabbage Chowder

INGREDIENTS

2.50 oz. Vegetable oil
50 oz. Onion, chopped
25 oz. Carrots, chopped
25 oz. Celery, chopped
2.50 oz. Garlic, minced
50 oz. Green cabbage, shredded
65 oz. Corned beef, cooked, cubed
1.25 qts. Beef Base, prepared
1 ea. Cream Soup Base, 25.22 oz. bag, prepared

INSTRUCTIONS:

1.In a large stock pot , over medium heat, heat oil. Sauté onion, carrots and celery for 10 minutes. Add garlic, sauté 2 minutes. Add cabbage, corned beef and beef base. Cook until cabbage is tender. Add Cream Soup Base, mix well and heat through. Taste and adjust seasoning with salt and pepper. Reserve warm.

2.To Plate: Serve 10 fl. oz. of Chowder in bowl.

88. Drive In Cheeseburger Chowder

INGREDIENTS

2.50 oz. Butter
5 lbs. Ground beef
25 oz. Onions, white, diced
15 oz. Pickles, dill, diced fine
26.25 oz. Ketchup
23.75 oz. Mustard
1 ea. Cream Soup Base, 25.22 oz. bag, prepared
5 qts. Cheese Instant Sauce Mix, prepared
  As needed Salt
  As needed Pepper
  As needed Croutons, sesame crusted

INSTRUCTIONS:

1.In a large stock pot, over medium heat, melt butter. Crumble and brown ground beef. Add onions, cook until tender and beef is cooked.

2.Add pickles, ketchup, mustard, Cream Soup Base and cheese sauce. Let simmer for 30 minutes. Taste and adjust seasoning.
3.Garnish with sesame crusted croutons.

89. <u>Heartland Hash-Brown Chowder</u>

INGREDIENTS

20 oz. Smoked bacon
35 oz. Ham, thin sliced, cut into fine strips
25 oz. Onions, white, grated
13.50 oz. Carrots, peeled, grated
13.50 oz. Celery, grated
2.50 qts. Ham Base, prepared
1 ea. Cream Soup Base, 25.22 oz. bag, prepared
5 lbs. Hash browns, grated
2 ½ Tbsp. Thyme, fresh, chopped
  As needed Kosher salt
  As needed Cracked pepper

INSTRUCTIONS:

1.In a large stock pot, over medium heat, render bacon until crisp. Remove bacon from pot (reserve for garnish). Add ham and frizzle until caramelized. Add onions, cook until done, add carrots and celery; sauté until tender. Add the ham base.

2.Add Cream Soup Base into pot. Mix well to combine. Add the hash browns and thyme. Simmer for 30 minutes, or until heated through. Taste and adjust seasoning.
3.Garnish with crisp crumbled bacon.

90. Rueben Chowder

INGREDIENTS

10 oz. Butter
30 oz. Onions, white, diced
30 oz. Bell pepper, green, diced
1 ea. Cream Soup Base, 25.22 oz. bag, prepared
5.25 oz. Dijon mustard
5 qts. Beef Base, prepared
5 lbs. Corned beef, cooked, shredded
2.50 lbs. Sauerkraut, rinsed, drained well
2.50 lbs. Swiss cheese, shredded
   As needed Croutons, rye bread
   As needed Swiss cheese, shredded

INSTRUCTIONS:

1.In a large stock pot, over medium heat, melt butter, sauté onions and peppers until tender. Add Cream Soup Base, mustard, beef base, and mix until smooth with a wire whisk.

2.Add corned beef and sauerkraut, stir and simmer for about 10 minutes. Stir in Swiss cheese, heat until melted. Taste and adjust seasoning.
3.Garnish with rye bread croutons and additional Swiss cheese.

91. Pepperoni Pizza Chowder

INGREDIENTS

8 oz. Pepperoni, diced
5 oz. Mushrooms, fresh, diced
28 oz. Tomatoes, canned, diced, drained
3 oz. Beef Base
1 ea. Cream Soup Base, 25.22 oz. bag, prepared
0.05 oz. Oregano, fresh, minced
1 tsp. White pepper, ground
16 oz. Mozzarella cheese, shredded

INSTRUCTIONS:

1.In a large stock pot, over medium heat, sauté pepperoni for 3-5 minutes. Add mushrooms and tomatoes, cook additional 5 minutes. Add beef base, stir well to combine. Add Cream Soup Base, oregano and white pepper, mix well and heat through. Stir in mozzarella cheese and heat until melted. Reserve warm.

2.To plate: Serve 10.0 fl. oz. of pepperoni Chowder in a bowl.

LAMB

92. Lamb and Lentil Chowder

Ingredients:
1 lb. ground lamb
1 onion, diced
2 garlic cloves, minced
2 cups chicken broth
1 cup dried lentils
1 cup diced potatoes
1 cup chopped kale
1 tsp. cumin
Salt and pepper
Olive oil
Instructions:

In a large pot or Dutch oven, heat some olive oil over medium-high heat.

Add the ground lamb and cook until browned, breaking it up with a spoon as it cooks.

Add the onion and garlic and cook until softened, about 5 minutes.

Add the chicken broth, lentils, potatoes, kale, and cumin and bring to a boil.

Reduce the heat and simmer for 25-30 minutes, or until the lentils and potatoes are tender.

Season with salt and pepper to taste and serve hot.

93. Lamb and Vegetable Chowder

Ingredients:

1 lb. lamb stew meat, cubed
1 onion, diced
2 garlic cloves, minced
2 cups chicken broth
1 cup diced carrots
1 cup diced potatoes
1 cup diced celery
1 cup frozen peas
1 cup frozen corn
1 tsp. thyme
Salt and pepper
Olive oil
Instructions:

In a large pot or Dutch oven, heat some olive oil over medium-high heat.

Add the lamb and cook until browned on all sides.

Remove the lamb with a slotted spoon and set aside.

Add the onion and garlic to the pot and cook until softened, about 5 minutes.

Add the chicken broth, carrots, potatoes, celery, and thyme and bring to a boil.

Reduce the heat and simmer for 20-25 minutes, or until the vegetables are tender.

Add the lamb back to the pot, along with the peas and corn, and cook for 5-10 minutes more, or until heated through.

Season with salt and pepper to taste and serve hot.

94. Spiced Lamb Chowder

Ingredients:

1 lb. ground lamb
1 onion, diced
2 garlic cloves, minced
2 cups chicken broth
1 cup diced potatoes
1 cup chopped kale
1 cup coconut milk
1 tsp. cumin
1 tsp. coriander
1/2 tsp. cinnamon
Salt and pepper
Olive oil
Instructions:

In a large pot or Dutch oven, heat some olive oil over medium-high heat.

Add the ground lamb and cook until browned, breaking it up with a spoon as it cooks.

Add the onion and garlic and cook until softened, about 5 minutes.

Add the chicken broth, potatoes, kale, coconut milk, cumin, coriander, and cinnamon and bring to a boil.

Reduce the heat and simmer for 20-25 minutes, or until the potatoes are tender.

Season with salt and pepper to taste and serve hot.

95. <u>Lamb and Barley Chowder</u>

Ingredients:

1 lb. lamb stew meat, cubed
1 onion, diced
2 garlic cloves, minced
2 cups chicken broth
1 cup diced carrots
1 cup diced potatoes
1 cup diced celery
1/2 cup pearl barley
1 tsp. thyme
Salt and pepper
Olive oil
Instructions:

In a large pot or Dutch oven, heat some olive oil over medium-high heat.

Add the lamb and cook until browned on all sides.

Remove the lamb with a slotted spoon and set aside.

Add the onion and garlic to the pot and cook until softened, about 5 minutes.

Add the chicken broth, carrots, potatoes, celery, barley, and thyme and bring to a boil.

Reduce the heat and simmer for 45-50 minutes, or until the barley and vegetables are tender.

Add the lamb back to the pot and cook for 5-10 minutes more, or until heated through.

Season with salt and pepper to taste and serve hot.

96. Moroccan Lamb Chowder

Ingredients:
1 lb. ground lamb
1 onion, diced
2 garlic cloves, minced
2 cups chicken broth
1 cup diced sweet potatoes
1 cup diced carrots
1 cup canned chickpeas, drained and rinsed
1/2 cup chopped dried apricots
1 tsp. cumin
1 tsp. paprika
Salt and pepper
Olive oil
Instructions:

In a large pot or Dutch oven, heat some olive oil over medium-high heat.

Add the ground lamb and cook until browned, breaking it up with a spoon as it cooks.

Add the onion and garlic and cook until softened, about 5 minutes.

Add the chicken broth, sweet potatoes, carrots, chickpeas, apricots, cumin, and paprika and bring to a boil.

Reduce the heat and simmer for 20-25 minutes, or until the vegetables are tender.

Season with salt and pepper to taste and serve hot.

97. Irish Lamb Chowder

Ingredients:

1 lb. lamb stew meat, cubed
1 onion, diced
2 garlic cloves, minced
2 cups chicken broth
1 cup diced carrots
1 cup diced potatoes
1 cup diced turnips
1 cup diced celery
1/2 cup heavy cream
1 tsp. thyme
Salt and pepper
Olive oil
Instructions:

In a large pot or Dutch oven, heat some olive oil over medium-high heat.

Add the lamb and cook until browned on all sides.

Remove the lamb with a slotted spoon and set aside.

Add the onion and garlic to the pot and cook until softened, about 5 minutes.

Add the chicken broth, carrots, potatoes, turnips, celery, and thyme and bring to a boil.

Reduce the heat and simmer for 45-50 minutes, or until the vegetables are tender.

Add the lamb back to the pot and stir in the heavy cream.

Season with salt and pepper to taste and serve hot.

98. Lamb and Leek Chowder

Ingredients:

1 lb. ground lamb
1 onion, diced
2 garlic cloves, minced
2 cups chicken broth
1 cup diced potatoes
1 cup sliced leeks
1 cup frozen corn
1 cup heavy cream
1 tsp. thyme
Salt and pepper
Olive oil
Instructions:

In a large pot or Dutch oven, heat some olive oil over medium-high heat.
Add the ground lamb and cook until browned, breaking it up with a spoon as it cooks.
Add the onion and garlic and cook until softened, about 5 minutes.

Add the chicken broth, potatoes, leeks, corn, and thyme and bring to a boil.

Reduce the heat and simmer for 20-25 minutes, or until the vegetables are tender.

Stir in the heavy cream and cook for 5-10 minutes more, or until heated through.

Season with salt and pepper to taste and serve hot.

99. Lamb and Mushroom Chowder

Ingredients:

1 lb. ground lamb
1 onion, diced
2 garlic cloves, minced
2 cups chicken broth
1 cup sliced mushrooms
1 cup diced potatoes
1 cup diced carrots
1 cup diced celery
1/2 cup heavy cream
1 tsp. thyme
Salt and pepper
Olive oil
Instructions:

In a large pot or Dutch oven, heat some olive oil over medium-high heat.

Add the ground lamb and cook until browned, breaking it up with a spoon as it cooks.

Add the onion and garlic and cook until softened, about 5 minutes.

Add the chicken broth, mushrooms, potatoes, carrots, celery, and thyme and bring to a boil.

Reduce the heat and simmer for 20-25 minutes, or until the vegetables are tender.

Stir in the heavy cream and cook for 5-10 minutes more, or until heated through.

Season with salt and pepper to taste and serve hot.

100. Lamb and Root Vegetable Chowder

Ingredients:
1 lb. lamb stew meat, cubed
1 onion, diced
2 garlic cloves, minced
2 cups chicken broth
1 cup diced parsnips
1 cup diced rutabaga
1 cup diced carrots
1 cup diced potatoes
1 tsp. thyme
Salt and pepper
Olive oil

Instructions:
In a large pot or Dutch oven, heat some olive oil over medium-high heat.
Add the lamb and cook until browned on all sides.
Remove the lamb with a slotted spoon and set aside.
Add the onion and garlic to the pot and cook until softened, about 5 minutes.
Add the chicken broth, parsnips, rutabaga, carrots, potatoes, and thyme and bring to a boil.
6. Reduce the heat and simmer for 45-50 minutes, or until the vegetables are tender.
Add the lamb back to the pot and cook for 5-10 minutes more, or until heated through.
Season with salt and pepper to taste and serve hot.

CONCLUSION

Chowder is a classic soup that has been enjoyed for centuries and remains a favorite among many. Its rich and creamy broth, combined with chunks of seafood or vegetables, make it the ultimate comfort food. With countless variations and ways to customize it, chowder is a dish that can be enjoyed by everyone. Whether you're a seafood lover or a vegetarian, prefer it thick and creamy or with a lighter broth, there's a chowder recipe out there for you. So why not try making a batch of chowder and discover why this beloved soup has stood the test of time.